MIND HIS BUSINESS, NOT THEIRS

Breaking Free From Self-Sabotage
Rising Above Opinions And
Embracing God's Purpose

— PHILIP DADA JR —

Copyright © Philip Dada Jr, 2025 Breakfree Forever Publishing

ALL RIGHTS RESERVED: No part of this book may be reproduced or transmitted in any form whatsoever, electronic or mechanical, including photocopying and recording any informational storage or retrieval system, without the express written, dated and signed with permission from the author.

Author:	Philip Dada Jr
Title:	Mind His Business Not Theirs
ISBN:	978-1-917815-15-4
Category:	Christianity / Business / Motivational

LIMITS OF LIABILITY/DISCLAIMER OF WARRANTY: The author and publisher of this book have used their best efforts in preparing this material. The author and publisher make no representation or warranties with respect to the accuracy, applicability or completeness of the contents. They disclaim any warranties (expressed or implied), or merchantability for any particular purpose. The author and publisher shall in no event be held liable for any loss or other damages, including (but not limited to) special, incidental, consequential or other damages. The information presented in this publication is compiled from sources believed to be accurate. However, the publisher assumes no responsibility for errors or omissions. The information in this publication is not intended to replace or substitute professional advice. The author and publisher specifically disclaim any liability, loss, or risk that is incurred as a consequence, directly or indirectly, of the use and application of any of the contents of this work. Printed in the United Kingdom.

DEDICATION

To my wife, Caitlin, there are seasons in a man's life when the world grows strangely dim, when the vision is cloudy, and the soul is weary with the weight of unseen battles. And yet, in every such season, you have stood steadfast, gentle, and gloriously strong.

You have mourned with me when sorrow sat in the corners of my heart, and you have rejoiced with me when heaven broke through the clouds. You have believed in me, not just as a husband, but as a man sent by God with purpose in his bones and fire in his belly. When I doubted, you reminded me of who I am. When I shrank back, you called me forward. When I spoke of this work you did not laugh, you agreed.

And on that golden summer afternoon in Elizabeth Park, when I told you I would write this book, it was your smile of quiet certainty, your words of gentle fire, that sealed it. Your affirmation that day lit something in me that has burned ever since. Without your courage to believe in me and in this calling, I do not know if these pages would exist.

So, thank you, Caitlin. My wife, my lover, my best friend, and fellow sojourner in all things eternal. This book bears my name, but it carries your fingerprints.

Yours forever,
Philip

FOREWORDS

My husband inspires me every single day with his resilience, strength of character and the unwavering heart he brings to everything he does. He is an outstanding man in every area of life who is endlessly determined to do God's will above all else. Watching him pursue his purpose with such dedication has been one of the greatest joys of my life. This book is a true reflection of the remarkable man I'm so proud to call my own.

Caitlin Dada (Wife)

Philip Dada Jr has loved God deeply from childhood, and his priesthood has been evident from an early age. He is kind, joyful, humorous, and warm-hearted, with a playful side when he relaxes. A natural leader, disciplined, focused, principled, and relentless in pursuit of his goals. He believes nothing is impossible. Bold, resilient, patient, and confident, he carries people with him everywhere he goes. He is truly a man of the people.

Cecilia Dada (Mother)

Barr. Philip Dada Jr is a man after God's heart intentional, disciplined, and deeply committed to his family, his calling, and the Kingdom. A focused and shrewd businessman, he carries a strong priestly grace and serves faithfully alongside his wife, Caitlin, his partner in life and ministry.

Philip Dada (Father)

I met Philip when we were both 18, and it was immediately clear that he was different. Even from such a young age, he showed himself to be a dynamic and creative leader, stewarding effectively everything he led. It has honestly been a privilege to have witnessed closely his continuous growth and evolution since then, and be able to call him my best friend. Whether it be ministry, business, marriage or anything else he puts his hand to, he has been a true example of integrity, reliability and what it means to be a God fearing man.

Michael Olasope (Best Friend)

CONTENTS

INTRODUCTION   7

SECTION 1: BREAKING FREE FROM SELF SABOTAGE   10

KEY 1: Awakening to the Father's Heart   16

KEY 2: Rediscovering Your Identity   32

KEY 3: Consecrating Yourself: 49
The Foundation of Fruitfulness

SECTION 2: RISING ABOVE OPINIONS   70

KEY 4: Mind Mapping   77

KEY 5: Partnering with the Holy Spirit   94

KEY 6: Excelling - Get The Work Done!   113

SECTION 3: EMBRACING THE PURPOSE OF GOD   133

KEY 7: Walking in the Father's Love   139

KEY 8: Finishing Well - Your Reward   157
From His Business

CONCLUSION   172

ACKNOWLEDGEMENTS   177

ABOUT THE AUTHOR   178

MIND HIS BUSINESS NOT THIERS

LATIN (VULGATE – JEROME'S LATIN TRANSLATION, 4TH CENTURY A.D.)

> *Et ait ad illos: Quid est quod me quaerebatis? Nesciebatis quia in his quae Patris mei sunt, oportet me esse?*
>
> Lucas 2:49, Biblia Sacra Vulgata

ENGLISH (DOUAY-RHEIMS, TRANSLATED FROM THE LATIN VULGATES)

> *And he said to them: How is it that you sought me? Did you not know that I must be about my Father's business?*
>
> Luke 2:49

INTRODUCTION

At just twelve years old, Jesus gave us a glimpse of his life's guiding philosophy:

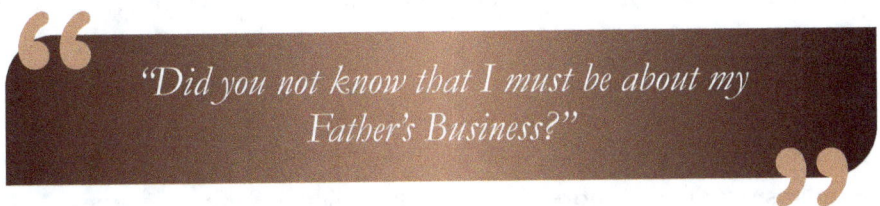

"Did you not know that I must be about my Father's Business?"

In that moment, He revealed a radical priority an unwavering on divine purpose that transcended societal expectations, family concerns and the pressures of culture. Jesus understood that life is short, the mission urgent, and the time to act is now.

If you are reading this, it is time to wake up. Time to break free from self-sabotaging habits that masquerade as normalcy. Time to silence the distracting opinions of men that pull you off course and steal your peace. Time to stop running in circles chasing validation, promotions or approval and start living on assignment fully engaged in the Father's business, not yours or theirs.

Modern life dazzles us with opportunity. Calendars overflow, ambitions grow, and the noise never ceases. Yet beneath the surface of busyness lies a restless ache a hunger for meaning that no achievement or accolade can satisfy. For many Christians, even those active in faith, this emptiness lingers. The question gnaws quietly: Is there more? Is there a deeper calling beyond my daily grind?

This book invites you to a vital shift in perspective one that will realign your heart heat, mind, and actions with the loving purpose of God. Many have been raised to see God as distant, demanding, or hard to please a distant ruler watching from afar. These distorted views breed fear, self-doubt, and distance, trapping us in cycles of performance and self-sabotage.

Mind His Business Not Theirs

But the true to God of scripture is a loving Father who calls us into partnership, who delights in relationship, and who offers us identify as His beloved children. When you grasp this, insecurity losses its grip. You no longer live to earn approval; you live because you belong. This freedom births courage to step into your calling and pursue it with all your heart, even when the world resists.

Still, many believers struggle with a sense of purposelessness. Society's definition of success wealth, status, productivity only deepens the disconnect. The endless pursuit of "more" leaves souls depleted. Without divine alignment, ambition fracture's identity and purpose, causing burnout, dissatisfaction and a sense of drifting. But there is a better way that bridges faith and vocation, worship and work, Sunday and Monday. Your true assignment is not about personal gain or fitting into a man-made expectation. It is about joining God's grand story with your unique role in advancing His kingdom.

Jesus' example at twelve challenges you to do the same: to prioritize God's business above all else. No matter where your calling unfolds whether in the boardroom, classroom, home or community your work carries eternal weight. Every act of faithfulness and every decision made in alignment with God's purpose contributes to a legacy that echoes into eternity. Ignoring this calling is costly. It drains potential, stifles growth, and breeds quiet regret. You were never created to live a borrowed life or chase someone else's assignment. When you neglect your divine calling, you begin to imitate rather than originate, compare rather than create, and settle rather than soar. That's where self-sabotage thrives, when you doubt your uniqueness, question your worth, and try to fit into a mold God never designed for you.
But embracing your calling liberates you. It silences the noise of comparisons and frees you from the tyranny of others' opinions. It gives you permission to walk confidently in your own rhythm of grace, knowing that God's fingerprint on your life is unlike any anyone else's. You must learn to confident in how your gift works, how your grace flows and how your purpose unfolds. You are not Mosses, called to lead through deserts and seas. You are not David called to slay goliath and govern Israel. You are not Esther, positioned in the palace for national deliverance, not Hannah, whose

tears birthed a prophet. Though you will learn from their faith, you are not called to replicate their path. You are a unique expression of God's creativity and power an original design carrying a specific assignment that no one else can fulfill.

To walk effectively in the Father's business, you must first accept this truth: Your difference is not a defect it's your distinction. God did not make a mistake in how He wired your personality, distributed your gifts, or ordered your journey. Confidence in your divine design is essential, because insecurity will always tempt you to play small or imitate others. But when you embrace who you are in Christ, your gift begins to flow freely, your voice grows clear, and your impact multiplies naturally. Walking in this confidence does not mean arrogance it means agreement. It means agreeing with what God has spoken. Over your life and refusing to downplay it for the comfort of others. It means accepting that your assignment might look different, sound different and move at a different peace and that exactly how it Is meant to be. When you stop trying to be someone else and start honoring who God called you to be, you step into the sweet spot of divine alignment. That's where grace flows without strain, where excellence becomes worship, and where purpose turns into legacy.

So, walk boldly in your lane. Celebrate the examples of Moses, David, Esther and all the patriarchs and matriarchs of the faith but never lose sight of the fact that you are God 's living epistle, an original creation of God, his workmanship for this generation.

As you journey through these pages, I encourage you to ask the Holy Spirit to cultivate within you a new resolve a passionate commitment to the Father's business that cannot be shaken. Invite His guidance to reveal your unique calling clearly, to strengthen your confidence in God's grace at work in you, and to empower you to overcome any temptation to self-sabotage or distraction by the opinions of others. Let this be a season of fresh awakening where you embrace your divine assignment with courage, joy, and unwavering faithfulness. The Father's Business is calling you may you answer boldly and fish well. Now, let's journey…

SECTION 1

BREAKING FREE FROM SELF SABOTAGE

There are battles that don't happen in the world around us, they happen in the quiet corners of our hearts. The truth is that many of us aren't fighting external enemies; we're fighting ourselves. We're not losing because opportunities are scarce, because resources are limited, or because people doubt us, we're losing to the voices inside that tell us we're not enough, not ready, not worthy. This is the tragedy of self-sabotage. It's subtle, often unrecognisable, and disguises itself as personality traits, coping mechanisms, or what we've been conditioned to believe is "just the way I am." Self-sabotage builds on one side and tears down on the other. It's the tendency to pray for growth yet run from the environments that challenge us to mature. It's saying "God, use me," but shrinking when He opens the door. It's carrying dreams while secretly believing they are out of reach.

For years, I lived this cycle without even realising it. Growing up, I developed a deep need for approval. I wanted to be liked, to be accepted, to be seen in ways that reassured me that I belonged. That need began to shape how I showed up in the world. I became the joker. No matter how serious or significant the moment, I would find a way to make light of it, to laugh, or to redirect attention with humour. When great opportunities came, instead of standing confidently, I would retreat behind laughter as a shield. On the surface, people enjoyed my presence. They found me charming, funny, likable. But underneath, that humour quietly became a prison. I was downplaying my own potential to make others comfortable, unknowingly eroding my credibility and disqualifying myself from doors I could have walked through.

It did not stop there. When insecurity ran deeper, I sought escape in patterns that I now recognise as destructive. Things like pornography and cycles of shame became temporary reliefs from a deeper pain, the pain of not feeling enough. I was searching for comfort in the wrong places, trying to fill a void that only the Father's love could satisfy. Externally, my life seemed fine. People saw a young man who could joke, smile, and interact easily. Internally, I was at war. I carried false identities "the funny one," "the likable one," "the one who never gets angry" all of them costumes hiding a son who had yet to fully understand the Father's heart for him.

Mind His Business Not Theirs

The Bible gives us many examples of this internal struggle. Jonah ran from God because he feared man's opinions and the scope of God's calling. Peter denied knowing Jesus because he feared rejection from others. Even David, a man after God's own heart, wrestled with insecurity and guilt in the Psalms. These stories remind us that self-sabotage is not unique to our modern experience; it is timeless. It emerges when we let fear, shame, or a need for approval outweigh the voice of God. It took me years to realise that the problem was not around me, it was within me. The thoughts, habits, and beliefs that kept me small were fruit of a deeper root: disconnection from my identity in Christ. When we don't know who we are as God sees us, we live a life shaped by other people's expectations. We make decisions based on insecurity rather than intimacy. We create patterns to protect our pain instead of surrendering it to God for healing. Self-sabotage is often the shadow of an unacknowledged identity, the gap between who we think we are and who God has called us to be.

Science helps us understand why this is so powerful. Psychologists tell us that humans are wired for approval. Our brains release dopamine when we feel accepted and withdraw when we feel rejected. This is a survival mechanism; an ancient wiring that helped early humans stay connected to the group. But that wiring can also work against us spiritually. When we live dependent on approval, we are enslaved to the very thing we cannot fully control: other people's opinions. Neuroscience also shows that repeated patterns of negative thought create neural pathways, literally training our brains to expect failure, inadequacy, or shame. In essence, self-sabotage becomes a habit that rewires us over time, making us feel trapped in a cycle that seems impossible to break. Research in cognitive behavioural psychology has demonstrated that thought patterns dictate emotional response and behaviour, confirming that when we allow fear, doubt, and false beliefs to dominate our minds, our lives mirror that inner chaos. But something changed when I began to awaken to the Father's heart. When I realised that His approval was not something to earn but something I already had through Jesus, something shifted inside me. The pressure to perform, to prove, to be liked, began to lift. I started to see myself differently. I discovered that living consecrated, set apart for God's purposes, was not a burden but a gateway to freedom. As I embraced my identity in Christ, I began to experience a new kind of fruitfulness.

What had once been cycles of frustration became cycles of growth. The shame that once held me captive began to dissolve, and my mind and heart were renewed. Scripture reinforces this reality in multiple places. 2 Corinthians 5:17 says that anyone in Christ becomes a new creation. Ephesians 2:10 reminds us that we are God's workmanship, created for good works prepared in advance. Romans 8:1 declares that there is no condemnation for those who are in Christ. These verses are not just words on a page; they are active forces. When I began to meditate on them, confess them, and internalise them, they reshaped my perception of myself and my potential.

Breaking free from self-sabotage is not primarily about behaviour modification. It is about rediscovering who you truly are. It is about moving from striving to resting in God's love. It is about recognising that your value is not determined by what you do or what others think, but by who you are in Him. It is about stepping into the reality that when you are aligned with your true identity, your life begins to bear fruit naturally. This is the essence of consecration: surrendering every part of yourself to God, not to earn approval, but to live fully as He intended.

Historical examples also show how internal belief shapes external success. People like George Washington Carver, who overcame poverty and racial prejudice, or Harriet Tubman, who risked everything to lead others to freedom, demonstrate the power of inner conviction rooted in a higher purpose. They did not rely on the approval of those around them. They were guided by a vision, a calling, and a deep inner alignment with truth. In the same way, when we align ourselves with God's heart and walk in our identity in Him, we begin to rise above the invisible chains that hold us back.

Even modern research supports this principle. Studies in psychology show that self-efficacy, the belief in one's own ability to succeed is directly linked to resilience, a positive mental health, and goal attainment. When we cultivate an accurate sense of our God-given identity, our confidence becomes anchored in truth rather than circumstance or opinion.

Neuroscientists also show that gratitude, meditation on positive truths, and reflection on accomplishments reshape the brain's neural pathways, increasing mental resilience and emotional stability. In essence, aligning our minds with God's truth rewires us for success, peace, and spiritual fruitfulness.

In my own life, the transformation was gradual but undeniable. I began to notice cycles of self-sabotage and old jokes that diminished serious opportunities, destructive escapes into shameful patterns, tendencies to hide behind humour or likability, slowly dissipating as I internalised my identity in Christ. I began to pursue excellence without fear of what others would think. I started to consecrate my time, my thoughts, and my choices, intentionally aligning them with God's purpose. And I began to see fruit. Opportunities that once seemed out of reach opened naturally. Relationships grew healthier. My mind became a place of clarity rather than chaos.

I also began to notice patterns in Scripture that mirrored my experience. Joseph was sold into slavery, falsely accused, and imprisoned. Yet his steadfast faith and understanding of God's purpose in his life allowed him to rise above betrayal and rejection, ultimately saving nations. Moses, despite being hesitant and fearful, embraced his identity as God's chosen deliverer, walking into a leadership role that initially felt impossible. Paul, once a persecutor of Christians, found his identity in Christ and became a vessel for worldwide transformation, unshaken by the scorn of society. In each case, God's truth within them overrode the opinions, doubts, and obstacles around them. They are living proof that self-sabotage can be overcome when we anchor ourselves in divine identity.

Breaking free from self-sabotage is not a one-time event; it is a process. It requires patience, intentionality, and surrender. It requires understanding that what you carry inside, your beliefs, habits, and identity, ultimately determine your external outcomes. When you learn to trace the roots of your thoughts, examine the lies you believe, and anchor your worth in God's approval rather than man's, you step into a life of freedom. You begin to experience the fullness of who God created you to be. You begin to walk in peace, confidence, and purpose, no longer manipulated by fear, shame, or insecurity.

In this section, we will explore three keys to breaking free from self-sabotage. We will examine how to uproot the lies that limit you, how to rebuild your identity on the truth of God's Word, and how to realign your life with the purpose. He has prepared for you. Until you master what is happening within, nothing lasting can be built without. Self-sabotage is not simply a habit to break or a behaviour to correct.

It is a misunderstanding of your identity, a disconnect from the Father's heart, and a cycle that only the truth of God can interrupt. When that truth takes root in your life, everything begins to shift, and fruit begins to grow where once there was only frustration.

KEY 1
AWAKENING TO THE FATHER'S HEART

Cease striving for approval - begin thriving, for you belong, forever, to the Eternal Father

Philip Dada Jr

More than half of adult's report feeling a persistent sense of emptiness or lack of purpose despite outward success in their careers and personal lives. Many chase promotions, accolades, or achievements only to find that the satisfaction fades quickly, leaving a deeper longing unanswered. This struggle isn't just about ambition or drive, it reveals a missing connection to something greater, a calling that offers true meaning beyond temporary accomplishments . For countless believers, the difference between a life drained by obligation and one filled with joy lies in understanding God not as a distant judge, but as a loving Father inviting us into His heart and purpose. This chapter explores why awakening to that relationship transforms how we see ourselves, our work, and our role in God's kingdom every day.

God the Father Unveiled: Embracing a Loving Relationship

Most people form their first thoughts about God through early experiences and the traditions they grew up in. Many carry images of God shaped by difficult relationships with authority figures, especially fathers who were missing, angry, or unapproachable. Some, like me recall being in church as children, feeling tense under the stern gaze of a Sunday school teacher, quietly promising themselves never to step too far out of line because God, they were told, always watched and judged. Others lived in homes where affection and affirmation were rare, so they easily map those memories onto their faith, envisioning God as distant or harsh rather than tender and present. These distorted images leave lasting scars, making it difficult to believe that God desires a real, close relationship. When God is seen only as a cosmic enforcer, any intimacy or trust with Him is choked out by a sense of fear and 'never-enoughness'.

Such misperceptions cause many to keep God at arm's length, avoiding meaningful conversations with Him and hiding their faults out of shame, afraid that disappointment or punishment is just behind the next mistake. People raised with the message that God's love must be earned often carry deep insecurity and skepticism into adulthood, even if they attend church or serve on ministry teams.

These wounds can grow into spiritual fatigue, anxiety, and the nagging suspicion that faith is mostly about obligations and avoiding wrath not about true relationship or transformation.

In sharp contrast, the Bible paints a far richer and more compelling picture of God as a loving Father. The story of the Prodigal Son stands as one of the clearest revelations of the Father's heart. Jesus tells of a young man who, after wasting every resource and dignity, returns home overwhelmed by guilt. Yet far from greeting his son with condemnation, the father races to him, embraces him, and restores everything the son thought was lost, a vivid sign that God eagerly receives and forgives, even those who fall hardest. In Jesus' own ministry, He often calls God "Father," teaching His followers to approach God not as groveling servants, but as sons and daughters invited to ask, seek, and trust boldly.

Scripture employs ample imagery to bring the tenderness and faithfulness of God to life. The psalmist describes God as a fortress, shield, and stronghold - one who lifts up rather than beats down, who carries and sustains instead of abandoning His people. The prophet Isaiah presents God as both mighty and nurturing, whose care can be compared to a mother's embrace, providing safety and comfort without fail. Such passages break through the fog of past hurts, inviting even those wounded by broken images of fatherhood to discover the truth of God's character. This God disciplines with love, not with rage; He corrects to heal, not to wound. He remains faithful, never capricious, and extends mercy fresh with each new day This understanding flips the script on a transactional approach to faith, where religion becomes a checklist and performance is valued above connection. Too often, striving to meet every expectation either to please God, a pastor, or a parent leads to emptiness, obligation, and burnout. Consider a leader who never asks for help or shares honest struggles, fearing rejection or the collapse of an image. While outwardly successful, their spiritual life feels hollow. In contrast, experiencing God as a loving Father makes transparency safe. Faith blossoms when honest conversation replaces ritual, and prayer becomes a warm exchange rather than fearful duty.

When believers anchor their identity in the Father's unconditional love, a profound sense of belonging takes root. Security no longer depends on performance or status but flows from the knowledge that each person is fully accepted as a child. This security grants courage in leadership, resilience under pressure, and freedom to serve generously without fear of inadequacy or burnout.

Leaders can risk, forgive, and encourage others because their confidence draws from being loved, not from achievement alone.

For many in the business or ministry world, achievement offers moments of satisfaction but often leaves an aching emptiness once the crowds fade, goals are met, or deals are done. All the recognition in the world cannot fill the void that comes from living apart from the Father's love and purpose. The deepest fulfillment, belonging, and peace come only from embracing God as Father, a relationship that grounds and sustains a life that impacts and endures. The journey becomes less about striving and more about resting in the Father's goodness, pointing us toward a wholeness the world cannot substitute

A Crisis of Purpose in Modern Life: Finding Lasting Meaning

A person rooted in the assurance of God's fatherly love will inevitably sense a growing tension when chasing meaning in a world overflowing with empty promises. It is striking how many adults, even those who claim success in the eyes of their peers, describe an aching void beneath their ambitions. The pursuit of influence, position, or accolades can become a treadmill one promotion leading to another, a string of accomplishments dimming quicker than anticipated. People pour themselves into work, imagining that diligence or recognition will fill the cracks in their identity, only to find the next milestone disappointingly hollow. Stories abound of talented professionals outpacing others on the corporate ladder yet confessing to exhaustion or a creeping sense of futility. Joy evaporates when the fruits of labour remain unanchored to God's higher design.

No matter how earnestly someone chases validation or financial gain, lasting fulfillment slips away when ambition is self-powered.

The workplace becomes a microcosm of this crisis.
Imagine the high-achieving leader who meets every goal but goes home numb, burned out by the pressures that come with chasing a definition of success that continually shifts. Or consider the employee who receives a long-awaited bonus, only to discover their sense of emptiness remains. These scenarios play out across industries and incomes. Labor alone, detached from God's meaning, fails to provide a secure sense of belonging or enduring satisfaction. Instead, over time, the cycle of striving without eternal roots produces fatigue and sometimes a sense of being lost. The reward for years of concentrated energy plaques, salaries, a reputation-turns out to be a poor substitute for the joy found at the intersection of calling
and relationship with God.

Beyond work, culture amplifies the crisis by defining success through possessions, popularity, or image. People internalise these scripts, convinced that appearance or assets are proof of worth. Advertisements and social platforms parade the rewards of wealth and achievement, urging everyone to compete in a game where the rules favor outward markers but overlook the desires of the soul. Many adults learn too late that filling the garage or bank account cannot settle the deeper longings for meaning, love, and purpose. This disappointment is not limited to those chasing luxury; it stirs in those who simply want security or recognition. When the narratives of culture guide our ambitions, we are prone to disillusionment precisely because these markers ignore the hunger for real connection and significance.

Mind His Business Not Theirs

Even those who manage to reach the heights outlined by society's standards often admit to a sense of disconnect. It is not uncommon for celebrated executives and respected professionals to quietly admit that something vital is missing. Their days are full, but their hearts are restless. This sense of restlessness is a signpost. Biblical wisdom recognises this dilemma:

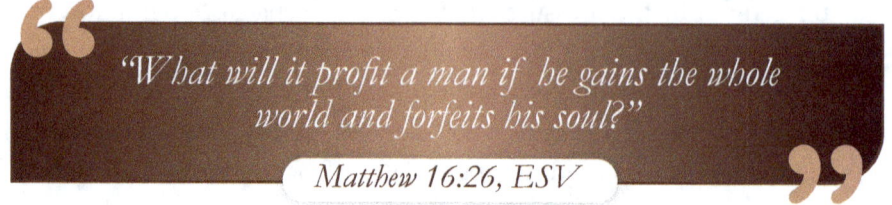

> "What will it profit a man if he gains the whole world and forfeits his soul?"
>
> Matthew 16:26, ESV

The questions asked in the quiet moments "Does this really matter?" "Does this work bless anyone?" "Am I living for something that outlasts" Surface because achievement divorced from purpose cannot answer them. The impact is visible in the rising tide of burnout, anxiety, and resignation that moves through boardrooms and break rooms alike A higher way unfolds by exchanging self-centered goals for God-centered ambitions. When the energy that once fueled comparison and competition is redirected toward God's unique design, daily activity becomes sacred. A Christian business owner, for example, may shift from maximising profits to building a workplace culture that honors integrity and nurtures people. A teacher may discover fresh passion in connecting lessons with a vision to shape lives for God's glory. A parent can approach each conversation with a larger view, recognising the home as a space where God's love is modeled and multiplied. Practical discipleship breathes life into every domain not by erasing ambition but by drawing it into alignment with God's mission.

True purpose and fulfillment are never found in fleeting forms of success; they become available when every pursuit is directed by the knowledge that one is called, chosen, and beloved by the Father. This identity infuses ordinary actions with significance and reorients desire toward what lasts. Jesus Himself demonstrated this: His youthful preoccupation was not proving Himself, but in attending to His Father's business, revealing a way of living in which direction, satisfaction, and peace converge through perfect focus on God's will (Moss, 1999). The invitation to follow this example stands open, promising to resolve the crisis at the heart of modern ambition.

The Son's Example: Jesus at Twelve Prioritising Divine Purpose

Many adults spend years chasing accomplishments only to discover an emptiness that worldly success cannot fill. A promotion finally arrives, but the moment fades. The business launches, but something restless persists beneath the surface. People often realise that ambition without deeper purpose begins to feel hollow, like chasing after wind. There are seasons when even the best resume or public applause does not quiet the ache to live for something truly lasting. This hunger for significance pushes us to look beyond fleeting achievements and ask: "What am I really here for?" The search for meaning demands more than relentless striving. It asks for a connection to God's greater story - a story that breathes value into our work, our relationships, and our influence.

This tension between worldly achievement and inner significance mirrors the moment when Jesus, at the age of twelve, stayed behind in the temple. The scene is layered with intensity and wonder. Imagine the busy, echoing halls of Jerusalem's temple during a major festival, filled with the hum of debate and the fragrance of incense. In this sacred space, Jesus sits among the most respected teachers of His day. He listens intently, asks probing questions, and shares insights so deep that all who hear Him are astonished. These scholars see a boy but encounter wisdom far beyond His years. Jesus' family searches anxiously, not fully understanding His actions, but He patiently explains

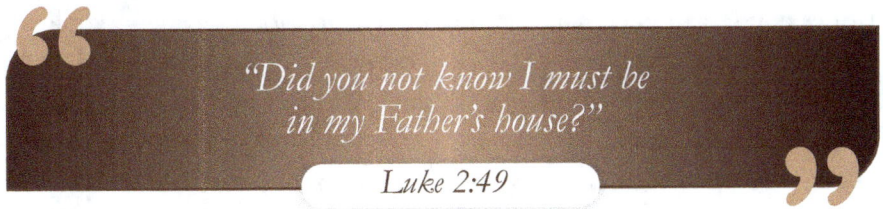

> "Did you not know I must be in my Father's house?"
>
> Luke 2:49

Mind His Business Not Theirs

In this moment, Jesus shows clarity of purpose that defies any expectation tied to His age or life stage (Luke 2:40-52 - Growing up God's Way, n.d.).

Cultural tradition expected Jesus to follow His parents' home. The community valued conformity, respect for family, and learning a trade ideal rooted in centuries of Jewish identity. Yet, His response shifts the paradigm: God's calling sometimes carves a path that others do not comprehend (Luke 2:40-52). Jesus' devotion to "His Father's business" offers more than an example of precocious youthfulness. It reveals that spiritual certainty and dedication are not things we stumble upon in later years or after acquiring titles and influence. The pursuit of purpose begins wherever we are, whether we are young adults charting unknown territory, mid-career professionals wondering if our efforts matter, or leaders wrestling with fresh responsibilities. Jesus' early awareness challenges us to ask: Are we pursuing ambition, or are we pursuing assignment?

The wisdom of Jesus in the temple points to a practical reality for today's believers. Consider a young professional who resists unethical shortcuts in the workplace, even if it means less recognition. Imagine a father who chooses being a consistent presence at home despite opportunities for rapid career advancement. Picture a ministry leader who senses God guiding them in a direction that others may question. Each scenario reflects the courage to obey the greater voice, God's voiceover comfort or accepted custom. This obedience often feels misunderstood. Friends may see our choices as risky or short-sighted. Family may worry that our devotion to God's priorities comes at a personal cost. Yet, the call to God's business requires confidence that transcends popular opinion. It means standing firm in faith when compromising would be easier (Luke 2:22 Study Bible: When the Days of Their Purification according to the Law of Moses Were Fulfilled, They Brought Him up to Jerusalem, to Present Him to the Lord, 2025).

Jesus' commitment invites believers of every age to recalibrate our priorities. If certain activities or goals keep us from serving God's purpose, no amount of outward success will satisfy.

Begin by engaging scripture personally and consistently, letting God's Word anchor your perspective amid shifting ambitions. Seek wise, godly counsel from mentors who will challenge you to align your pursuits with biblical priorities. Honestly assess where you may have let comfort or routine overshadow obedience. Are there areas where you shrink back from radical generosity, humility, or truthfulness because you fear standing out? The path to meaning does not depend on age or position. It relies on fresh, ongoing willingness to put God's assignment first in decisions both large and small.

As modern disciples, every opportunity in a boardroom, classroom, or living room carries potential for kingdom impact. God's call is not a one-time event; it is a continuous invitation to invest our days in what truly matters. Let Jesus' choice in the temple awaken in us the courage to pursue His business with undivided hearts. Embracing this calling opens a life richer than any career milestone, giving every moment eternal weight and joyful purpose (Luke 2:40-52 - Growing up God's Way, n.d.; Luke 2:22 Study Bible: When the Days of Their Purification according to the Law of Moses Were Fulfilled, They Brought Him up to Jerusalem, to Present Him to the Lord, 2025).

The Mandate Defined: Living on Assignment Today

Awareness of spiritual purpose opens the door to a life shaped by concrete action, motivation, and direction that reaches beyond the surface of daily routines. The sense of being "about the Father's business" is not abstract but is lived out practically every day. When Jesus, even as a boy in Luke 2, was devoted to the Father's affairs, He demonstrated that living for God is not just an idea but an ongoing engagement of the heart, mind, and skill in real circumstances. For today's believers, this posture begins with understanding stewardship as a privileged relationship of trust and partnership with God.

Christian stewardship never resembles the drudgery of forced labor. Instead, it means being entrusted with resources, talents, relationships, and opportunities with the knowledge that every assignment, large or small, carries grace and purpose.

Mind His Business Not Theirs

Imagine the difference between someone overseeing a project merely to avoid criticism versus doing so with a deep sense of God-given responsibility. The first breeds anxiety, resentment, or burnout, the hallmark of slavery to duty. The second, rooted in stewardship, unlocks joy, energy, and faithfulness. Whether managing a team at work, budgeting at home, or leading a neighborhood outreach, stewardship transforms routine responsibility into worshipful trustworthiness. Each task becomes an entry in the Father's ongoing story of redemption, where our contribution is celebrated and eternally meaningful.

At the very heart of the Father's business is the call to expand His kingdom, not only through traditional ministry, but in every sphere where life unfolds. Honest work of every kind can serve as holy ground. The marketplace is not a place of spiritual neutrality; each decision, interaction, or project offers an opportunity to embody kingdom values. A supervisor who extends mercy to an employee, a business owner who models ethical choices in the face of profit temptation, the caretaker who meets urgent needs with kindness, all are building blocks of God's reign revealed on earth. Small acts, repeated daily, become the seeds from which hope, justice, and truth spring. The ripple effect turns seemingly ordinary believers into culture-shapers, quietly claiming public spaces for Christ through consistency and compassion.

These kingdom advances are never meant to be accomplished alone or in isolation. God's design for His "business" involves a beautiful, interconnected tapestry of gifts and callings. The Spirit equips each person with strengths, abilities, and perspectives that together reflect His creativity and wisdom. Our calling is not limited to one visible role but is discovered in the combined outworking of each individual's tools and passions. The accountant who manages finances with transparency, the artist who crafts beauty that points to divine hope, the caregiver who offers dignity to the vulnerable all fulfill roles the world needs. No assignment is too small; each is dignified by the fact that it serves the Father's purposes at a specific time and place. Understanding one's personal call involves both self-awareness and spiritual discernment.

Past experiences, unique life stories, and gifts form the backdrop against which each believer's current context comes alive. When Christians prayerfully recognise their gifts, they see new possibilities for serving their generation and addressing specific needs. Instead of chasing cultural definitions of success or comparing themselves to others, they learn to value their assignment be it in the form of leading, creating, mentoring, or meeting needs behind the scenes (Wax, 2014).

Living on assignment means waking up daily with the quiet conviction that every environment; boardroom, classroom, home, or street is a place to represent Christ and foster wholeness. An entrepreneur does not simply measure success in revenue, but in the flourishing of employees, clients, and the broader community. A teacher's daily investment in a struggling student becomes part of God's redemptive work, far beyond the metric of grades. Parents shaping their children, volunteers reaching the overlooked, friends offering counsel at critical moments, all of these are practical outworkings of saying yes to God's invitation. Prayerfulness saturates daily choices, keeping ambition subordinate to divine intent and opening doors for influence that human plans alone cannot achieve. The cost of ignoring this divine commission is the loss of meaning, and abiding peace that flows from purposeful living. Without a vision of the Father's business, even outwardly successful lives can lack lasting impact. The antidote lies not in withdrawing from ordinary life, but in embracing every detail as an expression of God's kingdom come, one act, one encounter, one faithful step at a time.

Healed by Love: How Jesus Restores Us to the Father's Heart and Frees Us from Self-Sabotage

There is a kind of ache that grows quiet over time, the ache of unused gifts, silenced voices, and unlived assignments. It's not always caused by laziness or rebellion, but often by fear, shame, and deeply embedded patterns of self-sabotage. We don't always realise it at first. The days blur into routine, and little by little, the flame of calling flickers under the weight of doubt. Yet, even when our courage falters, the love of Jesus does not. He does not turn away from our hesitation, nor is He repelled by our brokenness. Instead, He draws near, healing us with a love that does more than forgive.

It reconnects us to the Father's heart and empower us to live from that place. Jesus never asked for polished perfection, He called disciples full of flaws. Peter, impulsive and often uncertain, denied Him, yet was still called to feed His sheep. Paul, once Saul the persecutor, was transformed by grace and became a writer of legacy and letters. What changed them was not ambition or willpower, but the love of Christ breaking through their pasts and ushering them into the Father's embrace.
The same love is extended to us daily.

Many of us carry gifts and callings that have grown dusty with delay. A writer full of holy imagination keeps their pen capped, fearing the judgment of others. A leader shrinks back in meetings; afraid their voice will sound foolish. A young parent senses the call to pray boldly over their children but doubts that their words carry spiritual weight. These aren't stories of indifference. They are stories of wounds, sometimes from childhood, sometimes from failure, sometimes from lies long believed. Lies like "You're too much," "You're not enough," or "You'll never get it right." These lies take root in the soil of our souls and quietly choke out courage.

Psychologists tell us that self-sabotage is often not rebellion, but a misfired instinct for self-protection. When our nervous system registers risk, relational, emotional, or even spiritual, it can trigger avoidance. We delay, we procrastinate, we sideline ourselves not because we don't care, but because something deep in us whispers, "Don't try. Don't be seen. Stay safe." What's tragic is that this "safety" becomes a prison. We protect ourselves from disappointment, only to live disappointed. We silence ourselves to avoid rejection, only to experience the ache of invisibility. We run from our assignments, thinking we're escaping pressure, but we end up haunted by purpose unrealised.

But Jesus never lets us go quietly into regret. His love is too persistent for that. He comes to the self-sabotaging heart not with condemnation, but with compassion. He does not shout over our doubts; He whispers through them. His Spirit reminds us:

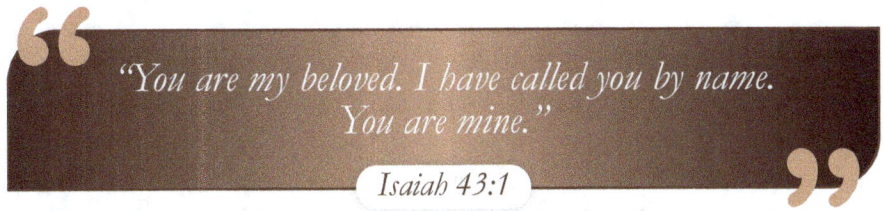

In that moment, everything begins to change.

His love realigns what fear distorts. Where shame says, "You're disqualified," Jesus says,

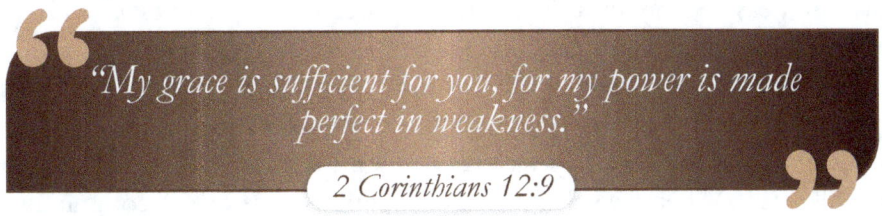

Where self-doubt says, "You're not ready," Jesus says, "Come, follow Me." He doesn't wait for our confidence to rise He calls us as we are. In the warmth of His love, we begin to unlearn the patterns of hiding. We begin to believe, not just with our heads but with our hearts, that we are not a mistake. That our voice matters. That our obedience counts.

This reconnection to the Father's heart is not abstract, it changes everything. We begin to see the world through the lens of belonging rather than survival. We are no longer striving to be worthy of our call; we are walking in it because we're already loved. From that place, courage grows, not the loud kind, but the steady kind. The kind that shows up even when the outcome is uncertain. The kind that says "yes" when it would be easier to stay hidden.

Mind His Business Not Theirs

And as we say yes imperfectly, vulnerably, we begin to live again. The teacher opens her door to mentor one younger soul, planting seeds of wisdom that will bloom long after she's gone. The father, once uncertain in his spiritual leadership, starts praying at the dinner table, trembling but faithful. The entrepreneur sees their business not just as a career but as a kingdom platform. They begin to move, not because they're fearless, but because they're rooted in love. The shift is subtle but seismic. No longer ruled by "what if I fail?" they are driven by "what if God moves through me?"

Scripture reminds us that we are not just participants, we are heirs. Romans 8:17 says, "If we are children, then we are heirs of God and co-heirs with Christ." That inheritance includes purpose, identity, and mission. But walking in it requires trust. It requires surrendering the belief that we have to have it all together to be used by God. It requires laying down the false protection of perfectionism and taking up the cross of obedience.

This is not easy. Sometimes the calling feels weighty. Sometimes we still hear old voices whispering discouragement. But when we stay close to the Father's heart, we're reminded that we don't carry the call alone. Jesus walked in perfect obedience not to burden us, but to show us the way and then empower us by His Spirit to walk in it, too. And yes, the cost of ignoring that call is real. When we sideline ourselves, others miss out. A community goes without a shepherd. A generation loses a voice it needs. The kingdom's witness is dimmed. But even then, grace still pursues. It's never too late to return. God can redeem years the locusts have eaten (Joel 2:25). He restores what we thought was too far gone. He brings beauty from ashes. He breathes on dry bones and calls them to rise.

This is the promise for all who have wandered, delayed, or doubted. The love of Jesus is not passive. It is active, healing, calling, and releasing. It finds us in the middle of self-sabotage and breaks the cycle with grace. It doesn't demand that we clean ourselves up, it invites us to come home. And from that home, we live. Not for approval, but from it. Not to earn God's love, but to express it.

So, if you feel the ache of an unused gift, if your heart has gone quiet with discouragement or doubt, listen again. Jesus is still calling. The Father's heart is still open. There is still time. There is still purpose. And above all, there is still love, a love that heals, restores, and sends you out into the world with courage you never thought you had.

Let this be the moment you stop shrinking back. Not because you're suddenly brave, but because His love is stronger than your fear. Let this be the moment you remember who you are: chosen, known, and called. And let that love pull you into motion not rushed or pressured, but faithful and free. Your assignment still matters. Your obedience still echoes. And the Father's heart is still beating with joy, waiting for your yes.

KEY 2

REDISCOVERING YOUR IDENTITY

*You don't work for belonging, you
work from it.
The Eternal Father calls you
His own.*

Philip Dada Jr

Have you ever felt uncertain about who you really are beneath the roles and responsibilities that fill your days? Do you struggle with questions like, "Am I truly accepted?" or "Where do I fit in God's greater plan?" Many Christians face these inner battles, wrestling with feelings of doubt, trying to measure their worth by what they do rather than who they are in Christ. When I got saved in 2012 there was a consciousness I had of who I had become in Christ but not much in my natural world changed immediately, so I struggled with feeling accepted around friends and family and this is the reality a lot of times In the midst of busy careers, leadership demands, and everyday challenges, it can be difficult to hold firmly to a clear sense of spiritual identity. How can we move beyond insecurity and performance-driven living to embrace the freedom and confidence that come from knowing ourselves as adopted children and co-heirs in God's kingdom? This chapter will explore those foundational questions and offer insight into recognising your unique place and purpose rooted in divine acceptance and love.

Royal Bloodlines and the Foundation of Identity

From the earliest pages of scripture, the language of adoption forms a deep thread through the story of God's people. In the New Testament, the apostle Paul brings this imagery into focus, declaring that those who trust in Christ are given

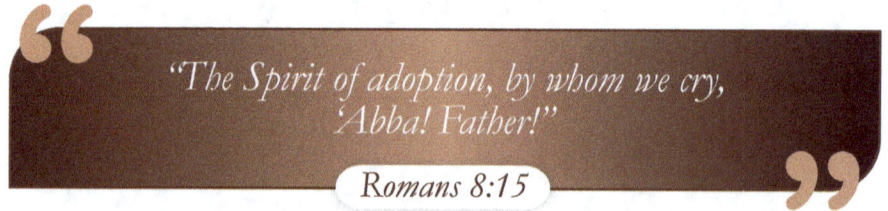

> "The Spirit of adoption, by whom we cry, 'Abba! Father!'"
>
> Romans 8:15

Here, the radical truth emerges, believers are no longer spiritual outsiders but cherished children, grafted fully into God's family. This adoption is not a mere legal arrangement or a distant association, by faith, every Christian is brought near, embraced, and welcomed with the same love that the Father lavished upon Christ. Just as adopted children in earthly families are granted the same privileges and inheritance as biological ones, spiritual adoption means that God delights to call you His own.

This new status as sons and daughters reshapes every aspect of identity. Earthly distinctions, social standing, cultural background, career achievements, fade in significance beside spiritual adoption. Through Christ's finished work, believers receive unconditional access to God's presence, daily guidance, and unfailing love. Ephesians 1:5 reveals that God "predestined us for adoption to sonship through Jesus Christ, in accordance with his pleasure and will." Adoption is God's joyful decision, not based on human merit or striving, but rooted in His steadfast love and sovereign grace. The invitation into God's family can never be earned, revoked, or reduced by any external force.

If adoption is the beginning, heirship is its fulfilment. Scripture proclaims that, in Christ, believers are "heirs of God and fellow heirs with Christ" (Romans 8:17). No longer are they merely forgiven or tolerated; they are entrusted with the riches of Christ's inheritance. This inheritance is both present and eternal: the gift of everlasting life, authority to walk in God's purposes, spiritual gifts, and the promise of a restored creation. With this status comes security, for nothing can separate those who are in Christ from the Father's embrace (Romans 8:38-39). Consider the parable of the prodigal son in Luke 15: when the lost son returns, he is not received as a servant but clothed with a robe and given a ring, a symbol of restored sonship and full participation in the family's privileges. Christ's work on the cross extends this same invitation to every believer, positioning them as co-heirs who are empowered to live boldly and purposefully within God's kingdom.

Still, embracing this truth is often met with profound inner resistance. Many believers wrestle with deep-rooted feelings of abandonment, spiritual insecurity, or the gnawing sense of never truly belonging. These emotions often stem from what is sometimes called the "orphan spirit", a mindset marked by striving, fear, and suspicion, where acceptance must be earned, and love seems conditional. The orphan spirit breeds restlessness and anxiety, leading Christians to measure their worth by productivity or the approval of others. True healing comes as the reality of God's fatherly love penetrates these wounds. Picture a leader driven by fear of disappointing God and others, constantly performing and hesitant to rest.

As this person receives the truth of adoption, resting in the assurance that nothing will break the Father's commitment, gradually anxiety gives way to peace, striving to sonship, and insecurity to quiet confidence.

The contrast between living for approval and living from acceptance becomes clear. Chasing the favour of God or people, believing identity is based on performance, induces weariness, perfectionism, and shallow relationships. In contrast, when grounded in God's unconditional approval, a believer moves from insecurity to boldness. Imagine a professional who exhausts herself seeking affirmation at work, constantly looking for validation to prove her significance. The fear of falling short suffocates creativity and stifles true impact. Yet, when her security rests in Christ's finished work, her service becomes genuine, her interactions sincere, and her sense of purpose unburdened by fear or comparison. Instead of anxiously labouring for love, she acts from a deep well of acceptance, confident in her place in the Father's family.

All attempts to erode Christian identity, from the orphan spirit or the lie of rejection, lose power when rooted in the unshakable truth of adoption and heirship. Scriptural promises such as John 1:12 ("to all who received him... he gave the right to become children of God") anchor believers against shifting emotions or circumstances. Personal stories of transformation remind us that these truths are not abstract, they are the foundation for healed hearts and fruitful, purposeful lives in God's kingdom.

Subtle dangers, however, still linger. Early attacks on our sense of belonging and value often arise when the enemy twists the truth about our adoption and inheritance, planting seeds of doubt in our minds and hearts. The next step is to recognise how such spiritual attacks infiltrate thoughts and daily experiences, distorting the foundation of true identity.

Warfare Over Self-Concept and the Power of Love

Understanding our adoption as God's children and our new standing as co-heirs with Christ brings both profound privilege and fresh challenges. The truth of being chosen and dearly loved brings to light the areas where insecurity, doubt, and striving often hold sway. When a believer encounters the depth of this favour, opposition grows more subtle. Feelings of unworthiness, the desire to prove value, and scars from rejection emerge more sharply against the light of divine acceptance.

The Erosion of Identity by Lies

One of the enemy's most effective tactics is the strategic sowing of lies that undermine spiritual self-worth. The first, and perhaps the most pernicious, whispers: "You are not enough." This thought surfaces in moments of failure, weakness, or comparison, causing hearts to question their significance in God's eyes. The second insists, "You don't truly belong," reviving memories of exclusion or distrust, alienating believers from both God and community. A third lie, "Your worth depends on your performance," shifts trust from grace to striving, leading to exhaustion and disappointment.

These accusations are designed to distort the believer's perspective. Scripture, however, counters each. The claim "You are not enough" is met by Ephesians 2:10: "For we are God's handiwork, created in Christ Jesus to do good works, which God prepared in advance for us to do." In times of feeling set apart or unwelcome, Romans 8:15-16 assures: "You received the Spirit of adoption. By him, we cry, 'Abba, Father.'" Even when driven by an urge to perform, God's promise in Galatians 4:7 prevails: "You are no longer a slave, but God's child; and since you are his child, God has made you also an heir."

Meditating on these truths have helped me personally in so many ways. It renews the mind and reshapes self-understanding. For example, when anxiety arises over being insufficient, declaring out loud, "I am God's handiwork, created with purpose," realigns the heart with God's reality. Returning repeatedly to the promises found in Romans and Galatians makes belonging and acceptance tangible, even in seasons of emotional isolation or spiritual dryness.

 ## Unmasking Comparison and Its Consequences

Comparison is a trap that often evades notice. It manifests quietly as believers assess their gifts, ministries, careers, or stages of life against those of others. A young professional in the church may envy the seasoned leader's influence. Parents might judge themselves relentlessly against families who appear more successful or organised. This cycle feeds dissatisfaction, insecurity, and resentment, blinding believers to their unique calling.

Scripture offers both caution and hope. Paul addresses this in 1 Corinthians 12:18-20, explaining that just as each part of the body is assigned by God, so each person's role and gifting have divine intention. No part is redundant or less valuable. Focusing on what God has entrusted personally discourages envy. Taking practical steps, such as listing one's own spiritual gifts and praying for clarity about their use, nurtures gratitude and expectation. Celebrating others' successes within the church strengthens unity and starves resentment.

Recognising this, believers grow when they invest energy into developing their own walk, serving faithfully with the abilities granted to them. Such mindfulness fosters freedom and genuine confidence. Trust emerges that God's plan is wise and His provision particular; vocations, influence, and even times of waiting are all expressions of personal care by a loving Father.

Strategies for Strengthening Identity

Recognise this, spiritual attacks rarely stop at the mind. Their reverberations affect daily behaviour, focus, and hope. Several practices serve as anchors:

Prayer:
Begin and end each day in conversation with God, specifically asking for discernment to recognise falsehood and courage to walk in truth. Invite the Holy Spirit to remind you of God's voice over any competing narrative.

Scripture Study:
Set aside time for slow, repeated reading of passages declaring God's love, and promises. Journaling how these verses apply to life situations deepens their roots in the heart.

Christian Community:
Engage intentionally with fellow believers who affirm, correct, and encourage. Small groups, accountability partnerships, and shared worship build resilience and perspective.

Faith-driven Action:
Actively serve according to one's gifts, even while wrestling with doubts. Movement cultivates assurance and grows roots deeper than mere sentiment.

As you apply the above you will find that there is a motivation that keeps growing in you to stay rooted in your God given identity and God's love. Motivation transforms when it springs from God's love rather than fear of failure. A believer secure in love volunteers with generosity, forgives readily, and approaches new opportunities without dreading imperfection. The anxiety of asking, "Am I doing enough?" is replaced by peaceful confidence in God's acceptance.

Receiving perfect love drives out fear and striving. Joy and freedom expand, making room for compassionate service and courageous living. As identity becomes deeply rooted in love, wounds from the past lose their power to keep the heart guarded. Vulnerability and forgiveness flow more easily, setting the stage for greater restoration and
healing yet to come.

From Brokenness to Wholeness: The Journey of Inner Healing

As you journey into your identity you will consistently be reminded that inner healing is necessary. You will discover that false narratives and harmful self-comparisons often have deep roots. Most people do not wake up one morning suddenly believing they are unworthy or that what others have defines their value. Underneath harsh self-judgments, there are memories, words, and events that have lingered long after their initial sting. At the heart of many struggles with identity is unresolved pain, moments of rejection, failure, loss, or shame left without healing. These quiet wounds shape how people see themselves and how they interact with others, often hindering genuine self-acceptance and faith in God's calling.

Old hurts have a way of muting God's voice. Baggage left unaddressed feeds doubt and fear and keeps hearts sceptical of grace. When pain is hidden, it festers. Spiritual effectiveness and growth become stunted, not because God is reluctant, but because old defences and hidden wounds act as barriers. Stepping into the fullness of being God's beloved requires facing the places within that ache for healing. Before someone can flourish or pour out love for others, the roots of their struggles must be seen and acknowledged.

The Power of Honest Recognition

Everything shifts when a person moves from avoidance to honest awareness. Acknowledgment is not about rehearsing old wounds or blaming others; it is simply seeing with clear eyes. David, Israel's shepherd king, modelled this in the psalms. He wrote with honesty about fear, sorrow, regret, and longing, turning even his pain into prayer. In Psalm 139:23-24, David prayed, "Search me, God, and know my heart; test me and know my anxious thoughts. See if there is any offensive way in me and lead me in the way everlasting." Recognition of brokenness is the entry point for God's healing work, not the end of the road. Refusing to name pain only delays restoration; honest confession welcomes the touch of God's transforming mercy.

The biblical story of the woman at the well (John 4) displays this principle. She had spent years avoiding her deepest wounds, living in shame and social isolation. Jesus met her not with condemnation but with understanding. He spoke the truth of her life, inviting vulnerability, and offered living water, a symbol of healing and renewal. Her willingness to acknowledge her need set her free to step into a new identity and purpose.

 ## Vulnerability as the Doorway to Transformation

Choosing vulnerability is not weakness or self-indulgence; it is the brave decision to remove masks and reveal reality. Many hide their struggles, assuming leadership or professionalism requires always being strong. In truth, transformation often begins with a leader seeking accountability, asking a trusted friend or mentor for prayer, or sharing uncertainty rather than pretending to "have it all together."

When a believer admits to a trusted confidante, "I am struggling with bitterness," or "This wound still hurts me," new avenues of healing open. Dependence on God grows out of these moments. Paul, who faced hardship and inner battles, wrote of his own

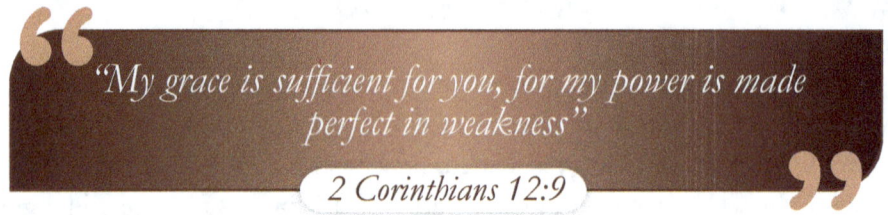

"My grace is sufficient for you, for my power is made perfect in weakness"

2 Corinthians 12:9

By refusing to hide their faults and needs, believers let grace become operative in places where self-reliance once failed.

 Forgiveness: Unlocking Spiritual Progress

I had to forgive my dad to begin embracing true healing. Growing up, he was always travelling for work and was only around on weekends, which left me with deep feelings of abandonment and a lack of male affirmation. Because of that, anytime I received affirmation from men, it carried so much weight that I sometimes placed it on a pedestal, almost to the point of idolatry. Through therapy and honest conversations with my wife, I came to see the root of this as a father wound. As I grew older, my dad became even more present, but opening up about this pain created space for God to begin healing my heart. Forgiveness allowed me to let go of resentment and start walking in wholeness.

No inner healing process is complete without forgiveness. Many believers seek healing yet find themselves bound by bitterness or chained by regret. Forgiveness extends beyond releasing others; it also involves releasing oneself from shame and self-condemnation. Clinging to past offenses or mistakes keeps hearts stuck, unable to move toward God's purposes.

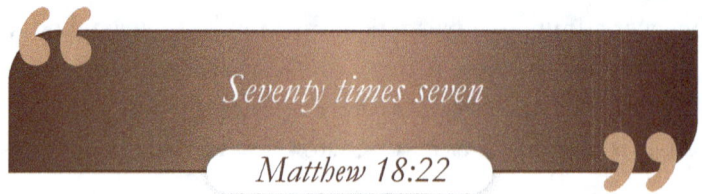

Seventy times seven

Matthew 18:22

Jesus taught forgiveness at the heart of His ministry. He told Peter to forgive demonstrating that mercy is not optional but intrinsic to a life rooted in grace. Forgiveness severs the hold of old pain. When a professional wronged by a colleague chooses forgiveness or a parent lets go of regret over past parenting mistakes, the grip of the past loosens. Forgiveness models Christ's mercy to the world, breaks cycles of personal and generational pain, and creates space for restoration.

 ## Restoration and Fruitfulness

Inner wounds, once healed, no longer define a life, but God does not erase the past; He repurposes it. Restored people hold empathy and greater resilience. A pastor once shackled by insecurity becomes a source of comfort to others who doubt their worth. An employee, healed from workplace rejection, leads with understanding and grace.

Restoration produces not only inner peace but equips one for meaningful service. God brings beauty from scars and uses what once broke a person to bless others. As hearts heal, unexpected gifts surface, patience, compassion, and the courage to step into new roles and challenges.

As healing brings restoration, believers recognise and celebrate their distinct roles in God's kingdom. Unique gifts once hidden under wounds begin to flourish, making space for contribution and purpose to thrive. The journey inward prepares the ground for the next steps, setting the stage for discovering the joy and meaning found in serving as a vital part of the body of Christ.

 ## Uniqueness Unleashed: Embracing Your Gifts and Role

A heart made whole can perceive and embrace its true worth. As healing restores what confusion and pain once clouded, people can begin to discern their genuine strengths and God-given callings. Wholeness is key to stepping forward without fear, using one's talents as intended rather than shrinking back in uncertainty.

When wounds are addressed and released, the voice of doubt fades, making space for the quiet assurance of being uniquely created and chosen.
God carefully designs each person with gifts that contribute to the richness and well-being of His church. This diversity is never random or secondary to some imagined ideal of sameness. Instead, every spiritual gift, natural ability, and calling is like a mosaic piece, essential to the full picture. Precisely because no two lives are carbon copies, the body of Christ flourishes. When people discover and accept their individual contribution, the entire community becomes stronger, vibrant, and more agile in fulfilling its mission.

 ## The Necessity of Diverse Gifts

Think of how different roles and gifts function in daily life. Someone with a knack for encouragement might send well-timed messages of hope, lifting others after a setback. A technically minded believer could volunteer on the audio team, helping worship and teaching come alive for a congregation. Another person's organisational skills might ensure a community event runs smoothly, blessing many in ways that are not always seen but deeply felt. Each task, whether greeting guests, providing a meal, or strategising for outreach, demonstrates the importance of every part working together. Without even one, something vital is missing.

Unity often gets mistaken for uniformity, as if following Christ means erasing personal distinctions. Yet, scripture points instead to unity rooted in shared purpose, not identical appearance or gifting. The early church thrived because apostles, hosts, teachers, and servants all joined their various strengths in a common cause. This principle stands today. When every person gives what only they can offer, the church becomes a dynamic, living body.

 ## Discovering Unique God-Given Traits

I first discovered my God-given trait to preach and speak publicly in 2014, when I was 19 years old studying at Coventry University in England. It came during a season of prayer, where God began to reveal to me that He had placed within me the ability to proclaim His word with clarity and conviction.

Mind His Business Not Theirs

What started as a personal prompting in prayer was soon affirmed by the community I was surrounded by at the time, as they consistently called on me to preach or teach the word of God. Looking back, I see how vital it is to discover the traits God has planted within us, because when we do, we not only find purpose but also become equipped to impact others in the way He intended.

Recognising your own strengths calls for intention. Begin by asking God in prayer to open your understanding to traits both obvious and hidden. Questions like "What work stirs my joy?" or "Where do others seek my help?" can reveal consistent patterns. Honest feedback from friends or mentors helps, as they often see what we overlook in ourselves. For example, someone who quietly connects newcomers at work might realise a gift for hospitality. A believer known for clear explanations during small group studies could be uncovering a teaching gift.

Keep a simple journal of moments when you sense energy and fulfilment. Over time, themes emerge. If you find yourself organising projects at work and home, perhaps administration is a calling to steward. If you light up when creating art or music, look for places these talents can encourage others. The goal is not to check boxes but to steward whatever God has entrusted, however humble or grand it appears.

Mind His Business Not Theirs

 Practical Methods for Understanding Your Calling

Write out compliments or encouragements you frequently receive from others.

Ask a trusted friend to honestly share where they see God at work in your life.

Set aside time in prayer, inviting God to bring memories and desires to mind.

Volunteer in areas of interest within your church, community, or company, observing which tasks feel natural and life-giving.

Reflect on childhood passions, as early joys often contain clues for adult callings.

Between the ages of 9 and 12, my mom would often tell me that I was going to be a public speaker. She even bought me a book on public speaking, planting a seed long before I could see it for myself. The irony, however, was that at that time I was painfully shy and insecure. I had developed a habit of mumbling my words, rarely speaking out clearly or enunciating properly . Yet, during that struggle, my mom saw something in me that I couldn't see in myself. Her belief gave me courage years later, when I finally discovered that one of my strongest gifts was indeed speaking. That early affirmation reminded me to lean into it, to pursue it intentionally, and to keep nurturing it. I'm still nurturing it today, and this experience has shown me the power of receiving feedback from people you value about your gifts and abilities and then taking responsibility to build on that truth until it blossoms.

Embracing Authenticity Over Imitation

It's easy to fall into comparison, wishing for someone else's strengths or feeling pressure to blend in. Yet, imitating others stifles the beauty of God's unique creative work. Suppose a believer with strategic vision ignores their gift in favour of a more visible public ministry. The body loses out on their ability to guide projects or solve problems. Or picture a quiet servant diminishing their role, thinking only vocal leader's matter. In truth, God weaves together both the spotlight and the silent labourer to reach hearts and fill needs.

Living authentically means functioning according to your divine design, not cultural expectations or exhaustion from self-effort. That might look like leading a prayer group, mentoring one person at a time, or caring for children in the nursery, each is sacred, and irreplaceable.

 ## The True Measure of Significance

Every role in God's kingdom carries weight. Significance isn't counted in stage time or applause but by faithfulness. An ethical businessperson shows Christ's love through honest leadership, modelling hope to colleagues and clients. A volunteer arranging chairs sets the scene for transformation. Both contribute to God's purposes, joined by shared devotion rather than identical methods.

As each person steps forward, fulfilling their unique calling, the effect is joy, deeper unity, and a church empowered for good works. The combined impact reaches farther than any single gift could alone. This is the heartbeat of kingdom purpose, many parts, working together, delighting God and blessing the world.

Bringing It All Together

Now that we understand the foundational truths of our spiritual identity, being deeply loved adopted children and co-heirs with Christ, we can face internal battles with courage, surrendering the lies that seek to steal our confidence and peace. Embracing our unique gifts and roles within God's kingdom empowers us to live boldly and authentically both in church and the marketplace, confident that our worth is grounded in grace, not performance. As we continue this journey of healing and discovery, I invite you to step fully into your calling, serving with faithfulness and joy, knowing that every contribution matters in God's purpose. With this clarity, we move forward equipped to impact our communities and workplaces, reflecting the love and authority given to us as members of His family.

KEY 3

CONSECRATING YOURSELF: THE FOUNDATION OF FRUITFULNESS

Holiness is not a cage but a crown, it is the wisdom that sustains true success

Philip Dada Jr

Have you ever wondered what it truly means to live a holy and consecrated life in today's world? Is holiness simply about following rules and avoiding mistakes, or is there something deeper that shapes every aspect of who we are? How can you remain faithful to God's calling amid the distractions and pressures of modern life, especially when work, family, and community pull you in so many directions? Many believers struggle with these questions, feeling burdened by expectations and uncertain how to cultivate a vibrant spiritual life that produces lasting fruit. This chapter invites you to reconsider consecration, not as a list of dos and don'ts, but as a daily journey of surrender, intimacy with God, and wise boundaries. It will help you discover practical ways to stay rooted in God's presence, guard your heart against distractions, and experience the freedom and joy that come from living set apart for His kingdom purposes.

Righteousness Consciousness, Not Sin Consciousness.

When I first got saved, one of the first areas God began to deal with in me was my lying tongue. Because I often felt different in groups and struggled with insecurity, I would sometimes lie just to fit in, not realising that my uniqueness was part of my destiny. Lying became almost automatic, something I did before even thinking. But when God confronted me, He showed me that I wasn't being smart by lying, I was lowering the standard of purity He had ordained for my tongue. In that process, He began to instil in me a consciousness of righteousness, not sin. Instead of being bound by the guilt of "don't lie, don't lie," I started to live with the awareness that I am the righteousness of God in Christ. That shift in identity empowered me to tell the truth, even under pressure, because I was no longer trying to fit in with people, I was walking in alignment with Him. This is how consecration is built: by minding His business, not theirs.

One of the most subtle but dangerous traps in the life of a believer is the entanglement of sin consciousness. It disguises itself as humility, discipline, or even spiritual maturity, but at its core, it is a mindset rooted more in shame than in grace, more in self than in Christ. When we are constantly aware of our failures, weaknesses, and shortcomings before God, we begin to build an identity around them.

Mind His Business Not Theirs

Our prayers become guilt-driven, our worship hesitant, and our confidence before God shaky. This is not the life Jesus died to give us. The finished work of Christ has redefined our relationship with righteousness. In Him, we are not trying to become righteous; we have been made righteous (2 Corinthians 5:21). That reality demands a shift, not just in theology but in identity and daily consciousness. Righteousness is not merely something we attain; it is something we receive. It's not something we work toward; it's the foundation from which we live. The believer's default posture should be one of righteousness consciousness, not sin consciousness.

Sin consciousness is the residue of an Old Covenant mindset where proximity to God was limited, where access to His presence required layers of sacrifice and priestly mediation. Under that covenant, sins were constantly remembered, year after year (Hebrews 10:1-3). But in the New Covenant, God says,

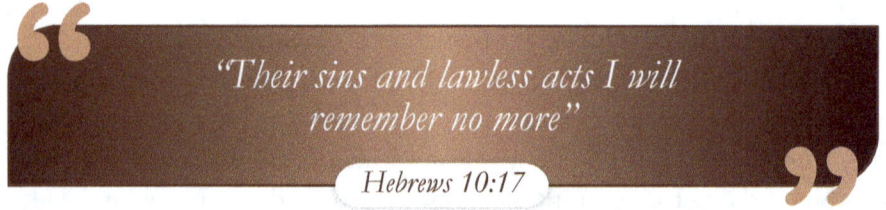

> *"Their sins and lawless acts I will remember no more"*
> Hebrews 10:17

The Cross was not just a payment; it was a declaration. The blood of Jesus did not cover sin temporarily; it removed it eternally for those who believe.

Yet many believers continue to live as if the Cross wasn't enough. We rehearse our failures, dwell on our weaknesses, and approach God with fear instead of boldness. But Hebrews 4:16 invites us to come boldly to the throne of grace, not because we are flawless, but because Christ is. Our confidence is not in our moral record but in His unblemished sacrifice. To be righteousness-conscious is not to be careless with sin, but to be more aware of Christ's victory than of our own shortcomings.

This doesn't mean we ignore sin. It means we no longer obsess over it as our defining feature. Paul acknowledged the struggle of the flesh in Romans 7 but didn't leave the believer there. In Romans 8, he triumphantly declares, "There is therefore now no condemnation for those who are in Christ Jesus." The progression is intentional, Paul shows us the struggle, then points to the solution: a life governed not by the flesh but by the Spirit. This life begins with the understanding that we are not condemned. We are free.

When a believer is sin-conscious, it often leads to either spiritual paralysis or performance-based religion. You're either constantly stuck in shame, afraid to come near God, or you're striving to earn your place with Him. Both are exhausting. Both rob us of joy, peace, and intimacy. But righteousness consciousness produces rest. It breeds confidence not arrogance, a humble confidence that says,

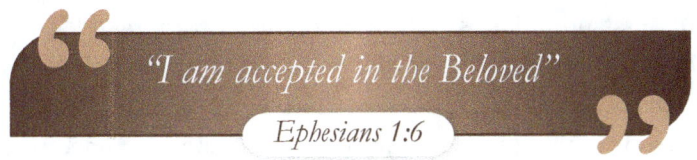

"I am accepted in the Beloved"
Ephesians 1:6

It empowers us to live holy, not to become holy, because we already are. The enemy knows he cannot remove a believer from salvation, but he will work tirelessly to remove their assurance. That's why righteousness consciousness is a form of spiritual warfare. When you believe rightly, you live rightly. Proverbs 23:7 says, "As a man thinks in his heart, so is he." If you think you are still a sinner barely scraping by, you'll live that way. But if you understand you are a new creation, righteous in Christ, empowered by the Spirit, you'll begin to walk in that reality.

This shift in consciousness also impacts how we treat others. Those who are sin-conscious often project their shame, becoming judgmental, legalistic, or harsh. But those who are righteousness-conscious become merciful, gracious, and full of truth. They remember they are recipients of mercy, not achievers of perfection. This allows them to love deeply, forgive freely, and lead humbly.

So, what does this look like practically? It's waking up daily and declaring who you are in Christ before the world has a chance to tell you otherwise. It's replacing "I failed again" with "I am being renewed day by day." It's looking at the mirror and seeing Christ's righteousness over your own reflection. It's worshipping from a place of access, not distance. It's praying with assurance, not anxiety.

Ultimately, righteousness consciousness restores us to the posture we were created for, fellowship with God. Not hiding behind fig leaves like Adam but walking boldly with the Father like sons. We are not imposters sneaking into a holy place; we are heirs, seated with Christ in heavenly places (Ephesians 2:6).

 Redefining Holiness in a Modern World

Many misunderstand holiness. It is often confused with rigid legalism, the belief that one's value before God is based on meticulous rule-keeping or outward appearances. Genuine consecration, however, can never be reduced to external compliance. The idea that true spirituality is attained through perfect observance of rules is not only misleading, but it also tends to breed pride or disillusionment. For some, striving for flawless behaviour produces self-satisfaction, as if their discipline grants superiority. For others, the constant sense of failure in not meeting an impossible standard, leads to discouragement and, at times, even giving up.

At its core, biblical holiness is not about a checklist of dos and don'ts. It flows from a heart fully surrendered to God. Legalism disconnects action from authenticity, whereas true consecration always springs from relationship, devotion to God who graciously calls His people to Himself. The apostle Paul's message about grace clarifies that genuine spirituality is found in the spirit, not mere adherence to the letter of the law. When living faith is reduced to lifeless rule-following, it produces external conformity without inward change, yet lives touched by God's presence are transformed from the inside out.

The difference becomes obvious in daily experience. Someone may rigidly observe every rule yet harbour bitterness, jealousy, or a critical spirit, proving that the internal life was never changed. By contrast, believers who cultivate intimacy with God see old patterns losing their grip and new character springing up: humility, patience, and graciousness. The fruitfulness of a consecrated life comes not from ticking all the boxes, but from ongoing surrender and love. Jesus Himself reserved His sharpest criticism for those who honoured God with their lips while their hearts remained far from Him. This internal foundation makes a practical difference, especially where cultural pressures challenge godly standards. Professionals may encounter subtle expectations to cut corners, exaggerate achievements, or prioritise popularity, while social life today is filled with voices urging compromise in values for the sake of inclusion. It's easy to spot overt temptations, but consecration is tested just as much by small, daily decisions. The key is to know one's own pressure points: for some it is the temptation to shade the truth, for others, to join in gossip or questionable humour, or to adopt questionable practices because "everyone else does it."

Combatting conformity begins with honest self-awareness and spiritual disciplines that anchor convictions. Praying regularly for discernment reveals how the world's current pulls at the heart, while scriptural meditation renews the mind and establishes clarity on right and wrong. Strengthening these foundations helps believers stand firm when "going with the crowd" would be easier. Developing a habit of meditating on truths from scripture infuses courage and clarity into routine decisions.

Accountability becomes essential. Having a trusted partner or spiritual mentor creates a space for honest reflection and encouragement. When personal resolve wavers, shared prayer and support make it possible to stay committed, even during opposition. Many find it helpful to start each day by reaffirming their dedication to God and asking Him for wisdom and endurance in tasks ahead. These habits nurture resilience and prepare believers for moments of trial, making compromise less likely.
There are countless stories, past and present, where radical devotion has transformed environments. A Christian employee in an industry known for shady practices chooses transparency and inspires colleagues to follow suit,

leading to a culture shift over time. A teacher, uncompromising in honesty and fairness, becomes a trusted voice among students and staff. Such individuals do not broadcast their convictions, but through quiet faithfulness, they become catalysts for change. Their influence is multiplied not only through big decisions, but by a steady pattern of integrity and kindness. These stories, echoed in church history, remind all that a consecrated life can bear fruit far beyond personal character.

Setting oneself apart comes with a cost. It can mean battling misunderstanding, disappointment, or even outright hostility, being bypassed for promotions, facing criticism for refusing to participate in questionable activities, or feeling isolated for not embracing popular values. Yet, the rewards are richer: knowing one's purpose, experiencing God's sufficiency in weakness, and developing an unshakable sense of worth anchored in divine approval, not fleeting social acceptance. Living out consecration in today's world is never easy, but it is possible. Practical habits, daily surrender, spiritual disciplines, regular repentance, and cultivating courage make holiness more than an abstract ideal. Through consistent devotion, believers develop the resilience and inner strength that sustain integrity and bring visible fruit: workplaces ripe with honesty, communities marked by compassion, and teams energised by conviction. Consecrated lives become living beacons, showing that transformation is possible, contagious, and deeply relevant in a world longing for authenticity.

 ## The Practice of Daily Surrender

The pursuit of excellence, authentic influence, and unwavering integrity as a Christian, demands something richer than outward conformity, it calls for a life shaped by daily surrender. This continual act is not about deprivation or rigid self-denial. Instead, surrender means waking up each morning ready to place every ambition, plan, and piece of personal identity in God's care. Choosing surrender frees believers from the noise of cultural pressures and shifting standards, allowing genuine relationship with God to shape their responses, choices, and impact in every context. Real holiness flourishes where surrender is more than a rule, it is a living practice that builds clarity, resilience, and profound strength

Morning Consecration Ritual

Back in my university days around 2013, I came across David's words in the Psalms:

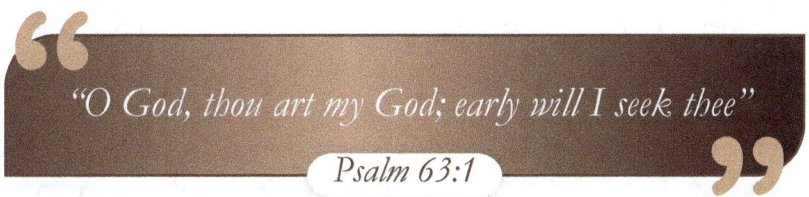

> "O God, thou art my God; early will I seek thee"
> Psalm 63:1

Not long after, I also noticed how the Gospels recorded Jesus Himself rising up early to pray:

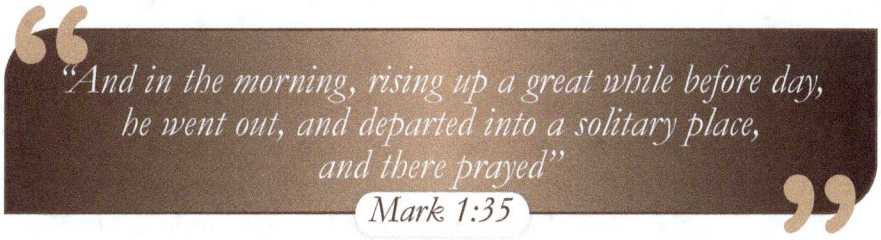

> "And in the morning, rising up a great while before day, he went out, and departed into a solitary place, and there prayed"
> Mark 1:35

Those verses struck a deep chord in me, and I sensed the Lord was inviting me to follow the same pattern. From that moment, I decided that seeking Him early, before the sun rises, would become a rhythm in my life.
It began as a simple practice in my dorm room waking up before classes to pray, to read the Word, and to sit quietly before Him. At first, it was discipline. But over time, it turned into delight. Morning after morning, I realised that when I gave Him the first part of my day, the rest of my day carried a sense of order, peace, and strength that I could not explain. Even after graduating and stepping into adulthood, I have continued this pursuit, carrying it with me into every season of life.

Mind His Business Not Theirs

Of course, there have been days when life demanded adjustments like when I had an early flight or after nights when I had to stay up very late. On those rare occasions, I would shift the time a little, but my heart remained steady: the Lord must be my first pursuit each morning. To protect this practice, I even made a small but powerful change in my routine. I began switching off my phone at night so that when I woke, my first gaze and attention would not be on social media or messages, but on Him. That one habit created space for me to grow in focus, hunger, and intimacy with God.

Looking back, I see how much this decision has shaped me. What started as a choice inspired by David and patterned after Jesus has now become my lifestyle. Over the years, the Lord has stretched my capacity and deepened my roots through these early mornings. Seeking Him before anything else has not only guarded my heart but also enlarged it, allowing me to walk with a greater sense of His presence in every area of my life.

Surrender begins before the first interaction or task. The first moments upon waking are an opportunity to present every need, schedule, and desire to God. This habit is deeply empowering, declaring dependence at the days outset and influencing all that follows. Start by designating a quiet space, even if only for five minutes. Stand or kneel, then either pray out loud or write a prayer, naming the specific plans, appointments, and emotions ahead.
A sample approach:

 Write or whisper, "Father, today I surrender my time, my conversations, and my goals to You. Let my actions honour You in every setting."

 Visualise placing each calendar commitment or concern into God's hands, pausing to notice any resistance or anxiety that arises.

 Ask for joy, wisdom, or strength for specific challenges, naming them with honesty.

 Repeat the prayer whenever new anxieties stir or interruptions come.

Mind His Business Not Theirs

For instance, a business owner might review the day's meeting list, holding up those relationships and decisions to God for guidance and patience. A parent could name a child's needs, trusting God's presence in school drop-offs or difficult conversations. This practice shapes the day's responses and builds confidence that every encounter can become an act of worship and trust.

 Journaling Your Commitments

There is transforming power in writing the very areas most resistant to surrender especially the ones tangled with fear, ambition, or uncertainty. Establish a journaling ritual, preferably after the morning consecration, to capture where surrender feels hardest.

- Open a private journal and list the worries, responsibilities, or outcomes you keep trying to control.
- For each, write a line such as, "Today I surrender my need to control outcomes at work," or "I give my fears about my family into Your care."
- Review previous entries daily or weekly, noticing shifts in patterns or emotions.
- Mark any areas that still feel tense, these are valuable places for deeper prayer and intentional release.

A teacher might write, "Today I give You my anxiety about results and trust You with my students' progress." Over time, flipping back through entries will highlight how surrendered areas begin to soften, opening toward peace as they are consistently trusted to God. This honest process invites God's presence into hidden corners rather than pretending strength where there is lingering struggle (candace.lane.official, 2025).

Accountability Check-Ins

Surrender thrives in honest community. Inviting another believer to walk alongside you prevents the isolation that leads to stagnation or blind spots. Begin by prayerfully considering a trusted Christian friend or mentor with whom you already share mutual respect. Reach out with a message such as, "Would you consider meeting weekly or biweekly to encourage one another and pray about specific areas we are learning to surrender?"

- Agree on a rhythm, perhaps thirty minutes over coffee, a video call, or voice messages.
- Each check-in, share one specific area where surrender felt fruitful or difficult, avoiding broad generalities.
- Exchange prayer points related to current challenges and victories.
- Encourage each other, offering reminders of God's faithfulness and insight from your own journey.

Imagine a stay-at-home parent and a friend sharing, "I surrendered my worry about finances this week; I found peace when I let go of my frantic budgeting." Both feel strengthened, not because of perfect progress but through real transparency and shared support.

 ### Celebrating Small Victories

Growth in surrender is most visible in the details. Watch for and record even the smallest moments where giving something to God brought peace, clarity, or a surprising breakthrough. Rather than vague gratitude, mark specifics, a resolved conflict, a calm moment in chaos, a sense of direction in the middle of confusion.

- Keep a victory jar, dropping in notes each time you recognise God's hand in surrendered areas.
- Text a brief appreciation to your accountability partner: "God helped me let go of disappointment in today's meeting. I felt free."
- Whisper a thanks to God each time you spot progress, however minor.

Consider a person who recognises their stress eased during an intense family discussion after praying their anxieties at sunrise. This awareness fosters momentum, shifting focus from what is lacking to the living evidence of God's presence and faithfulness. Each recorded victory builds courage for continued surrender and greater spiritual fruit

As these practices deepen, surrender ceases to be a burdensome duty and becomes a dynamic, ongoing relationship. Each deliberate step nurtures a "set apart" life. Soon, learning to remain close with God will energise every meaningful assignment, both sacred and secular,
that lies ahead.

 Intimacy That Fuels Assignment

Daily surrender and honest self-examination form the roots of a life that grows close to God. When a person surrenders their worries, desires, and doubts each day, they make space for God's nearness. This intentional opening of the heart allows intimacy to grow, not as a fleeting feeling, but as real partnership. The work begins in personal moments, laying down pride, inviting God's correction, and trusting Him with what lies ahead. Each daily act of turning to God shapes an environment where real connection and growth can flourish (King, 2024).

Prayer sits at the centre of this partnership. It is easy to think of prayer as a habit of asking or reciting words. While prayer certainly includes requests, its essence runs deeper. Prayer is a living dialogue, a place where personal thoughts and God's voice meet. Through this ongoing exchange, direction and fresh purpose enter every part of life, from home to workplace, from solitary tasks to complex assignments. For instance, imagine a business owner who faces a tough decision. Instead of relying on sheer expertise, this person pauses, seeks God with honesty, and listens. In this quiet space, unexpected answers and creative solutions can emerge, solutions anchored in values, wisdom, and discernment that go beyond what hard-driving effort alone can produce. Assignments become shared. Work flows not just from individual talent, but from connecting to God's strategy and presence. Tasks that once seemed burdensome become opportunities to experience God's power and leadership firsthand. Listening, especially in moments of stillness, is key to this kind of living. The rush of daily life and the noise of constant notifications risk drowning out God's gentle promptings. Intentional silence makes room for God's whisper to reach receptive hearts. Consider the ministry leader who chooses to sit quietly before each significant discussion. In these moments of peace, clarity and confidence grow. Next steps come into focus, not through anxiety or pressure, but through quiet awareness of God's guidance. Even five minutes of stillness can guard against impulsive choices and pave the way for wiser decisions. Rather than seeing silence as wasted time, it becomes the very space in which missteps are avoided, and energy is aligned with what matters most.

Engaging with specific scriptures can strengthen this ongoing closeness. Certain passages are especially powerful for reminding believers of God's faithfulness and presence. Meditating on the words of Psalm 23 brings comfort: "The Lord is my shepherd; I lack nothing." It nurtures trust in God's daily guidance. John 15, where Jesus describes himself as the vine and people as the branches, emphasises the life-giving power of remaining connected to Him. Philippians 4 encourages casting anxieties on God and resting in His peace. These passages do more than inspire. A professional facing workplace anxiety who meditates on Philippians 4 may find new courage for tough conversations or creative ways to handle stress. God's Word becomes an active, ongoing conversation, not a box to check. It forms a living bridge, deepening trust between God and the person seeking Him. Each moment spent with scripture becomes an invitation for God to speak, encourage, and guide.

Abiding in God's presence brings a noticeable difference to every area of responsibility. Abiding means resting in God's love, letting His voice shape priorities and plans. This posture leads to sustainable fruitfulness, results that emerge naturally out of connectedness with Him. Striving, on the other hand, relies solely on personal willpower and relentless performance. It leads to stress, fatigue, and results that often lack lasting impact. Imagine an entrepreneur who once worked themselves into exhaustion, always chasing the next achievement. Through learning to abide in prayer and God's Word, new ideas flow more freely. Rather than burning out, they discover joy, fresh vision, and real, lasting progress that blesses others. What changed was the source, moving from self-reliant striving to peaceful, purposeful partnership with God. Intimacy with God, then, does not simply make people feel better. It equips them with real strength, wisdom, and life direction for every assignment, at home, in ministry, or in the world beyond. When trusted and practiced daily, this closeness fuels lasting, meaningful impact. Even as this journey continues, threats and distractions are ever-present, quietly urging the need for vigilance to guard this foundation of intimacy moving forward.

 Guarding Your Heart Against Distraction

The challenge of maintaining intimacy with God grows sharper when distractions multiply and demand our attention. Digital technology, constant communication, and a rhythm of unending busyness can erode the clarity and depth of our communion with God. To thrive as consecrated, fruitful people, Christians are called not only to pursue closeness with the Lord but to actively protect their hearts and minds from the steady hum that steals spiritual focus. Guarding your heart is not just about avoiding obvious sin; it is about stewarding attention, choosing what occupies your inner world, and making space for what matters most before God.

Modern life operates at a pace and volume that can drown out the quiet voice of God. The allure of screens, the ever-present ping of notifications, and the expectation to be "always on" have real consequences, impacting not only spiritual well-being but also mental resilience and creativity. Technological clutter, if unrestrained, dulls our ability to think deeply, pray with focus, and notice the Spirit's promptings.

Mind His Business Not Theirs

The starting point for regaining clarity is simple but essential: eliminate unnecessary noise. This might look like setting a daily "technology fast," where all devices are silenced or put away for a designated period. A professional could turn off email and messaging notifications after dinner, reclaiming a pocket of evening quiet. Another practical guardrail is creating technology-free zones, perhaps the kitchen table or the first fifteen minutes of the morning. Even a brief, five-minute pause maybe while parked before heading into work can be an intentional pocket of silence to breathe, pray, and surrender the day. This practice of quiet disrupts the cycle of habit-driven responses and reorients the heart toward God's presence

Distraction is not just about noise, but about drift. The world's default is to fill every blank space with activity and entertainment, which silently reshapes what we value and pursue. Many find their days slipping by in a blur of urgent-but-unimportant demands, crowding out the consistent time and energy needed for those things that express God's kingdom priorities. Establishing priorities is thus crucial, a deliberate act of consecration. Christians are called to schedule their lives with intention, placing their deepest allegiances at the centre. This means identifying what matters most, prayer, worship, learning, serving, relationships, and giving these rhythms protected status in the weekly routine. Imagine the entrepreneur who sets aside daily non-negotiable time for Bible meditation before attending to the morning's emails, or parents who sanctify Sunday evenings for family prayer, refreshments, and sharing. These acts of purposeful alignment challenge the drift of culture and allow for a life that reverberates with kingdom fruitfulness.

No matter how well ordered a schedule may be, interruptions are inevitable. Meetings are delayed; children need attention; an urgent request interrupts quiet time. These moments test our resolve, but they also offer opportunities for spiritual growth. Dealing with interruptions requires a heart that is not just disciplined, but flexible and grace-filled. Instead of seeing these disruptions as obstacles, believers can view them as moments for holy detour, occasions to practice presence with God in the unexpected. Quick mental cues, or breath prayers, whispered lines such as, "Lord, meet me here," or the recitation of a favourite verse help recentre the mind.

The worker waiting for a conference call to begin could use those few spare minutes for silent prayer or reflection. Life's pauses become invitations for connection, not mere frustrations.

Underlying all these strategies is the call to spiritual watchfulness. Scripture encourages believers to be vigilant, to guard the heart above all else, and to stay alert to God's movements through the normalcy of daily life. Watchfulness is a form of holy attention, keeping the ears of the soul attuned to the Spirit's whispers despite the noise of responsibilities and demands. Journaling, asking periodic self-inquiry questions, and recording those moments where God nudges or offers clarity can train the heart to notice divine movement. For instance, a marketplace leader may sense a persistent thought to encourage a coworker, or a parent feels prompted to pause and pray for a child's emotional well-being. Training oneself to heed these moments preserves the vibrancy of intimacy and guards against a drifting, distracted heart

Learning to manage distraction is not a rigid practice of avoidance but a joyful discipline, a creative act that empowers Christians to live set apart amidst the noise. As each person grows attentive and creates distance from the chaos, they lay the groundwork for wise, loving boundaries, making room for God's voice and priorities to shape every part of life.

The Joy of Saying 'No'

People-pleasing begins subtly, growing into a deeply ingrained habit that quietly erodes spiritual calling, mission clarity, and inner peace. The pressure to keep everyone happy compels believers to take on more than they can handle, leading to exhaustion and frustration. Many Christians, desiring to reflect Christ's love, find themselves saying yes to every request, volunteering for additional church committees, covering extra work shifts, or sacrificing time intended for rest and family. What seems like devotion often masks a fear of conflict or rejection, making it difficult to say no even when boundaries are truly needed. Over time, this pattern shifts a person's focus away from God's direction and toward chasing others' expectations.

This cycle gradually blurs personal conviction, stifles honest self-assessment, and leaves the soul wide open to distractions that threaten to derail one's unique kingdom purpose (Sattgast, 2015).

Unchecked people-pleasing creates fertile ground for overcommitment. A spreading sense of guilt or inadequacy develops when declining requests, reinforcing the notion that personal worth is tied to constant usefulness or public affirmation. These fears can undermine authenticity, drawing believers away from trustworthy dependence on God. Living to satisfy the perceived needs of others replaces deliberate pursuit of God's voice and calling, sometimes leading to a shallow, anxious ministry, outwardly busy but spiritually depleted. In both church and professional settings, Christians who lack clear boundaries are prone to burnout, bitterness, and a sense of chronic overload that clouds discernment. Fears of disappointing supervisors, ministry leaders, or family members may keep believers locked in unproductive routines, unable to prioritise kingdom assignments over the tyranny of the urgent.

Principled boundaries begin with a clear-eyed look at the values and callings rooted in scripture. Identifying non-negotiable commitments means examining each sphere of life for areas prone to mission drift. For instance, a Christian professional may discern a boundary around not checking work emails after dinner, sheltering precious evening hours for faith development, relationship-building, or rest. Parents dedicated to shaping their children's faith might set aside one night each week for undistracted family discipleship, declining extra church meetings that crowd these sacred times. Ministry leaders may communicate the need for weekly Sabbath, respectfully reminding their congregations that rest is not self-indulgence but God's command and provision.

Articulating boundaries is most effective when handled with gentle directness and consistency. When a friend asks for help during an already full week, a believer might respond, "I care about you and want to help, but I also need to honour my commitments at home right now." At work, a supervisor might hear, "I appreciate this opportunity, but I won't be able to take on another project until next month." These statements not only draw lines but also signal respect for both parties, lowering confusion and resentment. Consistently expressing and maintaining boundaries protects time for spiritual practices, personal relationships, and creative endeavours that serve God's priorities rather than others' shifting demands.

Healthy boundaries do more than prevent exhaustion; they open space for joy and creativity. Every 'no' spoken in wisdom is a yes to something rich and life-giving. By declining overextension, believers gain freedom to pursue Bible study, prayer, crafts, music, outreach, or time in nature, any activity that deepens Christ-centred living. Stress diminishes as believers come to rely on God's sufficiency, rather than frantically guarding their own status. The sense of always being behind lessens, and margin appears for reflection, vision, and intentional movement in alignment with the Spirit. When former obligations drop away, clarity increases regarding where to steward energy and attention, a transformation marked by greater peace, focus, and resilience

Jesus provides the clearest example of boundary-setting for deeply purposeful living. Gospel narratives show Him leaving crowds who clamoured for more miracles, withdrawing to solitary places to pray. Even when needs abounded and expectations pressed in, Jesus sometimes did not meet every demand. His regular withdrawals protected His unity with the Father, refreshed His spirit, and clarified His mission. In the face of pressure, Jesus regularly made space for intimacy, discernment, and obedient action, choosing to disappoint human demands in favour of God's greater calling. He demonstrated that love is not measured by how much we do for others, but by how faithfully we follow the purpose God sets before us.

Following Jesus' pattern, believers find that principled boundaries are not selfish or harsh, but vital for living authentically before God. Declining requests can feel difficult, especially when people are genuinely in need, but saying yes to every demand ultimately hinders the ability to serve with integrity and power. By cultivating habits of boundary-setting, Christians characteristically preserve time, focus, and emotional health, making themselves available for Spirit-led assignments that have lasting impact. This practice releases them from striving, gently drawing them into daily dependence on God's wisdom and provision, a lifestyle authentically consecrated, effective, and full of joy.

 Bringing It All Together

Now that we understand holiness as a dynamic, daily surrender rooted in intimate connection with God, it's time to confront and break free from the patterns that keep us stuck, especially the quiet but crippling force of self-sabotage. No longer will we let fear, shame, or false narratives dictate our choices. The holiness we are called to is not about pretending to be perfect, it is about being fully present, fully surrendered, and courageously obedient to the One who calls us worthy.

Today, the call is clear: rise and shake off the delay, the doubt, and the distractions that have quietly numbed your passion and dulled your purpose. Embrace practical, Spirit-led habits -prayerful commitment each morning, honest self-examination, intentional boundaries, and vigilant spiritual guardrails. These aren't just disciplines; they are declarations of war against the lies that tell you youwre not enough, not ready, or too broken to be used by God. This isn't about behaviour modification. This is about reclaiming your identity and walking in the freedom Christ already won. You were never meant to live small, buried under the weight of your past or paralysed by fear of failure. You were made to live set apart - with joy, resilience, and holy fire bringing transformation into your workplace, your home, your relationships, and your community from the inside out.

So, moving forward, let this be your charge:
no more self-sabotage. No more shrinking back. Commit to cultivating rhythms of intimacy and integrity not because you have to earn God's approval, but because you already have it. Walk forward with clarity and courage and watch how a life surrendered to holiness bears fruit that outlasts you, fruit that shakes the kingdom of darkness and brings glory to God both now and for generations to come.

You're not disqualified. You're not too late. You are chosen. It's time. Step in.

SECTION 2

RISING ABOVE OPINIONS

The loudest voices in our generation are not always the wisest ones. We live in a world filled with noise, a world where everyone has something to say about how you should live, what you should do, and who you should become. The pressure to conform, to be liked, and to be accepted is stronger now than ever. Culture teaches us to measure our value by visibility, followers, and applause. But when your confidence is built on human approval, your peace will always be fragile. Rising above opinions is not about arrogance or rebellion; it is about alignment with God's truth. It is the art of silencing the noise of culture, critics, and even your own inner doubts, so that you can clearly hear and follow the voice of the Father.

The opinions of man can be one of the most dangerous prisons to live in. They don't bind your body; they bind your boldness. They limit how far you go, how freely you dream, and how authentically you show up. They cause you to second-guess divine instruction and to question the very things God has already confirmed to you. So many destinies have been delayed not because of demonic warfare, but because of the subtle fear of man, that constant concern with being liked, accepted, and understood. The fear of man makes you edit yourself, tone down your conviction, and dilute your purpose just to maintain approval from people who may never understand your calling.

I know this personally. Growing up, I was always different. There was something in me that wanted to go the extra mile while everyone else was comfortable doing the bare minimum. I wanted to be excellent in everything I did, but that drive often made me stand out, and standing out sometimes felt lonely. There were moments when I questioned whether my standards were too high or whether I was trying too hard. I remember trying to tone it down, to be more "relatable," to fit into the rhythm of mediocrity that surrounded me. But each time I did, I felt an unease in my spirit, like I was betraying something sacred inside me. It took me years to realise that this desire to push further, to reach higher, was not pride, it was God's pioneering Spirit at work within me.

Mind His Business Not Theirs

That's when I began to see that many of us are not simply "different", we are being developed. The discomfort we feel when we can't blend in is often evidence that God has set us apart. What you interpret as isolation might actually be consecration. What feels like rejection might be divine redirection. God doesn't call His leaders to blend in; He calls them to build what doesn't yet exist. The reason many believers struggle to rise above opinions is because they haven't yet recognised the leadership within them. The gift of leadership manifests in many ways, through ideas, creativity, conviction, or simply a refusal to settle. But when you are unaware of this divine deposit, you may mistake your uniqueness for a flaw rather than a calling.

Rising above opinions means choosing obedience over validation. It means understanding that as long as you are loved by God and walking in His will, you have nothing to prove. The love of the Father frees you from the need to perform. It silences the voices of doubt that tell you that you must be seen to be valuable or applauded to be successful. When you live from the Father's love, you realise that approval is not something to chase; it is something you already have in Christ.

You stop measuring yourself by the noise of men and begin to measure yourself by the still, affirming voice of God.

The story of Gideon reminds us of this truth. When God called him, Gideon didn't 'look' powerful, confident, or ready. He was hiding, unsure of his ability and overwhelmed by the opinions of those around him. Yet God addressed him not by what he looked like, but by what He saw in him: "The Lord is with you, mighty man of valour." That moment changed everything. God didn't need a crowd to validate Gideon's strength, His word was enough. Gideon learned that one with God is a majority. That's what it means to rise above opinions: to anchor your identity not in the voices around you but in the voice above you.

As believers, we must learn to silence the noise both external and internal. The greatest battles are rarely fought in the physical; they are fought in the mind. Not every thought that passes through your mind comes from God. Some thoughts are born of fear, others of pride, and many from insecurity.

This is why discernment is vital. The enemy's most effective weapon is not always sin, but suggestion. It's the subtle whisper that makes you doubt what God has already said.

In Genesis 3, before sin entered the world, deception entered the mind. The serpent did not force Eve's hand, he questioned her thoughts. "Did God really say…?" With that single suggestion, the clarity of God's word was replaced by confusion. From the very beginning, the battle for destiny has been a battle for thought. That is why Paul wrote,

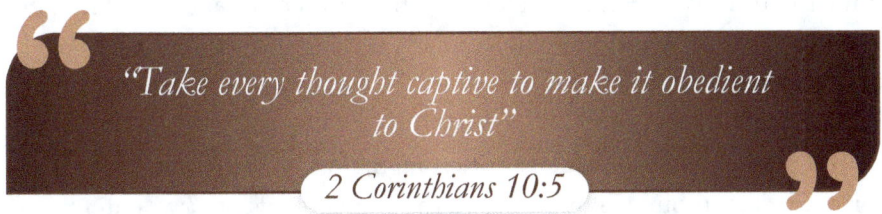

> *"Take every thought captive to make it obedient to Christ"*
> *2 Corinthians 10:5*

Every thought has a source, and every source has an agenda. Kingdom mind mapping is the spiritual discipline of tracing those thoughts back to their roots, identifying whether they are born of faith or fear, of the Spirit or the flesh.

When you begin to mind-map spiritually, you stop letting your thoughts control you and start governing them by truth. Romans 12:2 reminds us, *"Do not be conformed to this world, but be transformed by the renewing of your mind."* The Greek word for "transformed" is *metamorphoō* the same word used to describe Christ's transfiguration. This means that transformation doesn't start with your behaviour; it starts with your thinking. When your mind is renewed, your life begins to reflect the mind of Christ.

Even science affirms this principle. Neuroscientists have discovered that our brains are *neuroplastic*, meaning they can physically change based on what we repeatedly think, believe, and imagine. Toxic thoughts literally rewire the brain to create stress and anxiety, while meditating on truth and gratitude rewires it toward peace and creativity. Dr. Caroline Leaf, a Christian cognitive neuroscientist, has shown that renewing the mind through intentional thought patterns can reshape neural pathways.

Mind His Business Not Theirs

In essence, when Scripture tells us to "be transformed by the renewing of your mind," it's not just spiritual poetry, it's divine neuroscience. The Word of God literally reforms the architecture of your brain. That is why the believer must guard their mental environment. The thoughts you allow to dwell in your mind will eventually shape your emotions, your decisions, and your destiny. Proverbs 23:7 says, *"As a man thinks in his heart, so is he."* The mind of Christ must govern how we think, decide, and respond. When you bring your thoughts under His authority, confusion is replaced with clarity, fear with faith, and doubt with divine confidence. The more your thoughts align with God's Word, the more immovable your confidence becomes, not because you think more highly of yourself, but because you think more accurately according to Heaven's truth.

And yet, mental renewal alone is not enough; it must express itself in how we live, work, and build. This is where the principle of *excellence* enters. Excellence is the discipline of doing God's work with precision, passion, and consistency, even when no one is watching or applauding. It is not about perfection; it is about devotion. Excellence is the outward manifestation of an inward order. When your mind is renewed, excellence becomes natural, because your spirit no longer tolerates mediocrity.

Daniel was an excellent man. Scripture says,

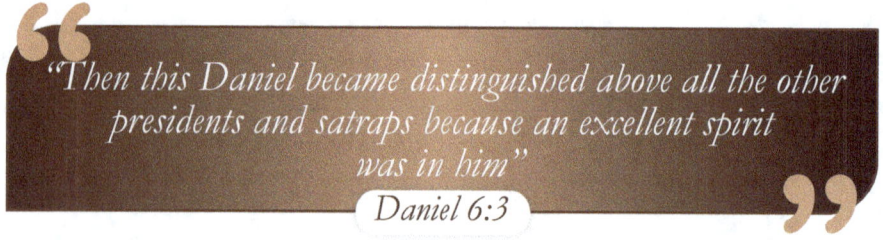

> *"Then this Daniel became distinguished above all the other presidents and satraps because an excellent spirit was in him"*
> Daniel 6:3

Notice it wasn't simply his skills or education that set him apart; it was a spirit. Excellence is spiritual before it is practical. It begins when you understand that everything you do is unto the Lord. Colossians 3:23 says, *"Whatever you do, work at it with all your heart, as working for the Lord, not for human masters."* When you live from that revelation, you stop performing for the opinions of men. Your excellence becomes worship.

Throughout history, the most transformative men and women understood this. Michelangelo spent four years painting the ceiling of the Sistine Chapel often lying on his back for hours in painstaking detail not because the world demanded it, but because he believed that "the true work of art is but a shadow of divine perfection." Johann Sebastian Bach signed every composition with the initials *S.D.G.* - *Soli Deo Gloria,* meaning "To God Alone Be the Glory." They weren't striving for fame; they were stewarding excellence as a form of worship.

Modern research echoes the same truth. Psychologists studying "flow states" have found that when people immerse themselves in meaningful, focused work, the kind that demands excellence, their brains release chemicals that heighten creativity, focus, and fulfilment. Excellence, therefore, doesn't just glorify God; it transforms us. It develops mental clarity, spiritual discipline, and emotional stability. When you commit to doing all things well, you align with the very nature of God, who does nothing halfway.

When you understand this, you stop lowering your standard to fit in with others. You stop apologising for doing things with care, depth, and distinction. You realise that excellence is not pride, it is humility before a perfect God. It is saying, "Lord, You are worthy of my best." Whether you're building a business, raising a family, writing a book, or leading a ministry, your excellence becomes a reflection of your revelation of Him. As you rise above the opinions of men, renew your mind, and walk in excellence, you will begin to see that you were never meant to blend in with culture, you were meant to set a standard for it. When you silence the noise of others and align your thoughts and work with Heaven, you become unstoppable. Your confidence becomes unshakable. And your life becomes a living testimony that when a believer truly *minds His business,* every other voice fades into insignificance.

When you embrace that truth, you no longer wait for external validation to do great work; you simply move in obedience with what God has placed within you.

Mind His Business Not Theirs

In this section, you'll discover that rising above opinions isn't about becoming louder than others, it's about becoming clearer within yourself. It's about learning to walk in the Father's love until His voice becomes the only one that defines you. It's about learning to discern your thoughts, align your mind with truth, and uphold a standard of excellence that reflects the Kingdom. My prayer is that as you journey through these principles, you'll find freedom from the weight of opinions, the paralysis of comparison, and the limits of external validation. You'll learn that the only approval that matters is the one that comes from Heaven, and that when your heart is fixed on the Father's business, no opinion on earth can slow you down.

KEY 4

MIND MAPPING

The mind renewed becomes a garden of God- lies uprooted, truth planted, and fruitfulness inevitable.

Philip Dada Jr

The mind of Christ is universally excellent, and as I've grown into that consciousness while building my fashion brand, Philip Dada Jr, I've come to see that His mind is not just about purity, but also about excellence, beauty, and glory. As an entrepreneur, I realised that creativity, innovation, and the pursuit of mastery are not separate from my faith, they flow directly from the mind of Christ within me. In Him, there is no mediocrity, no compromise, only a standard that reflects heaven's brilliance on earth. Even Solomon, with all his celebrated wisdom, did not carry more than a fraction of the weight of Christ's mind. That revelation has reshaped how I build, reminding me that to think with the mind of Christ is to build with eternal excellence that the world cannot deny.

Renewing the Mind Through Truth

Renewing your mind is crucial for your destiny because the battles that determine the course of your life are first fought in your thoughts. Paul says, *"it is with the mind we serve the Lord"* which means that even before our actions or words line up with God's will, our thinking has to be brought under His rule. An unrenewed mind, weighed down by lies, insecurities, or old patterns, will always distort how you see yourself and what you believe you can achieve. That's why destiny is never just about talent or opportunity, it's about alignment. When your mind is renewed by the Word, you begin to see yourself as God sees you, and this changes everything about how you approach your life, relationships, and assignments.

The truth is that the mind is a spiritual garden. If left untended, weeds of fear, deception, and limitation will choke out your growth. But when God is allowed to cultivate it, your mind becomes a place of abundance and fruitfulness. As I've learned in my own journey, The mind renewed becomes a garden of God - lies uprooted, truth planted, and fruitfulness inevitable. A renewed mind doesn't just keep you from sin; it gives you vision, boldness, and the capacity to build in excellence. That's why in building my fashion brand, I realised that every step of innovation and every expression of beauty first flowed from how I allowed God to shape my thinking. When you guard your mind, saturate it with truth, and submit it to the Spirit, your destiny cannot help but manifest because the seeds God has planted in you will always bear fruit in due season.

Negative thought patterns, sometimes called strongholds, do more than discourage or distract, they function like invisible barriers, setting limits on how much of God's power and purpose you experience. These mental strongholds are often old habits of thinking, shaped by life experience, disappointment, repeated failure, or even inherited beliefs from family and culture. Without realising it, a person may accept lies such as "I'll never be free from fear," "I'm not worthy of God's love," or "Change is impossible for people like me." Even faithful Christians are not exempt; left unchecked, these thoughts gain territory until they drive behaviour, block spiritual growth, and keep believers from trusting God's promises (Rom 12:2; That is why you must take seriously the work of identifying what fills your mind. If you delay, the strongest arguments against faith continue quietly, restricting your growth and your freedom).

The Bible makes plain that believers must *"not conform any longer to the pattern of this world but be transformed by the renewing of your mind."* Renewing the mind is not an optional add-on for the Christian's walk; it is the means by which God's truth erases old scripts and uncovers what He has planned for your life. Strongholds do not dissolve by wishing them away or waiting for time to heal your thoughts. Scripture connects spiritual transformation directly to mind renewal (Rom 12:2; 2 Cor 10:5). If Satan cannot steal your salvation, he is content to keep you in cycles of self-doubt and negative thinking because then you see only your weakness, not God's power. That is why identifying and confronting these hidden beliefs is crucial. This is spiritual warfare, and the battleground is your thought life (*Transformed Living*, 2014).

Speaking God's word aloud is more than spiritual discipline; it is how you reclaim authority over your mind. When someone speaks truth from scripture consistently and audibly, that truth counteracts hidden lies and gradually establishes itself as the guideline for decisions and responses. Consider the believer who wakes up anxious, haunted by thoughts like "I am not safe" or "things will get worse." Opening God's word, they read, *"God has not given me a spirit of fear, but of power, love, and a sound mind."* They choose to say: "I reject fear. God gives me power, love, and self-control." Saying it out loud, even if a whisper, even if trembling, begins to rewire the brain's habitual reactions. Each repetition carves a new mental path.

Over time, where anxiety once dominated, new responses form, rooted in faith. This verbal confession is not wishful thinking or empty ritual. It is taking God's narrative as your own and refusing to let negative self-talk define your identity

The process of identifying and rejecting lies builds on confession. Here is a practical method any believer can use:
Self-Help Steps for Breaking Strongholds

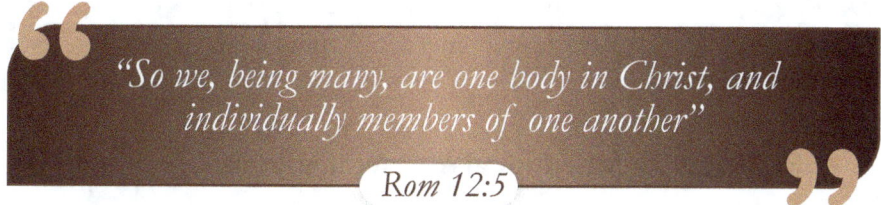

"So we, being many, are one body in Christ, and individually members of one another"
Rom 12:5

1. **Write down persistent troubling thoughts.** When you notice thoughts that generate fear, shame, or despair, pause and record them. Example: "I fail at everything important. I am not good enough."

2. **Look up specific scriptures that contradict the lie.** Use a concordance, digital Bible, or trusted study guide to find verses that speak God's truth to the issue. For someone feeling unworthy:

For feeling powerless:

3. **Cross out the lie and write the scriptural truth next to it.** Draw a line through the negative statement and write, "In Christ, I am accepted and equipped with spiritual weapons."
4. **Pray a simple prayer to renounce the lie and accept the truth.** Example: "Father, I reject the lie that I am not enough and accept your word that I am a member of Christ's body. Renew my mind with your truth."

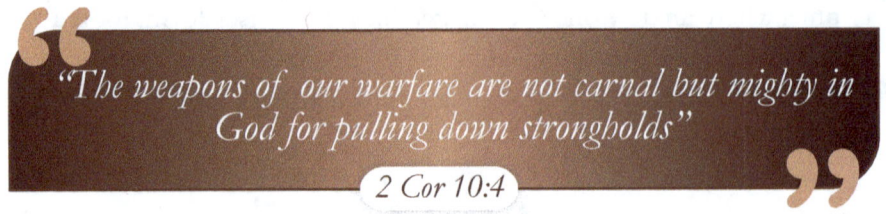

"The weapons of our warfare are not carnal but mighty in God for pulling down strongholds"
2 Cor 10:4

This work transforms daily living. Imagine facing recurring doubts "Nothing good ever happens for me." You discover Psalm 23:1, *"The Lord is my shepherd; I lack nothing."* You cross out the old thought and put God's promise in its place. Then you speak it and pray it, until God's perspective grows stronger than the old pattern.

 Creating a Daily Scriptural Affirmation Routine

Building new thought patterns requires ongoing reinforcement. Choose one truth each week that addresses a personal struggle. Write it on an index card. For example, if insecurity is the issue, Romans 12:2 can become your anchor: *"Be transformed by the renewing of your mind."* Each morning and night, say this verse aloud, affirming the truth "God, you are renewing my mind. I am not trapped by old patterns." Carry the card with you, review it during moments of stress, and mark how your reactions shift over seven days. This simple, deliberate habit anchors your identity and builds a spiritual defence. What was once automatic discouragement gives way to courageous, faith-filled responses.

Shifting your thoughts is only the beginning, transformation sets the stage for seeing God's purposes that reach beyond circumstances, as the next section will reveal. Holding to God's truth prepares you to direct your vision and energy toward the goals of His Kingdom, **Vision Beyond the Natural.**

Spiritual vision is not about what the eyes can see but about how faith transforms perception. Faith acts as a kind of spiritual sight, enabling us to see God's realities and promises, even when our outward circumstances seem to say otherwise. Drawing upon Hebrews 11:1, *"faith is the assurance of things hoped for, the conviction of things not seen"*. Without this cultivated faith-vision, Christians remain locked in momentary setbacks rather than walking into the endless possibilities available through God's kingdom. For example, someone experiencing a job loss might only see defeat or fear a diminished future, yet with spiritual vision, that same person recognises an opportunity for God to provide, redirect, and even expand their calling in unpredictable ways. This sight becomes more than mere hope; it transforms hope into an active and confident expectation that draws God's intervention into the real world (Kingdom of God – Matt Tommey Mentoring, 2025).

Spiritual vision demands a mindset that looks beyond immediate evidence and developments. This is not passive resignation or denial; it is an intentional pursuit that actively trusts God to guide, provide, and transform. When believers respond in faith, obstacles become launching pads for new spiritual adventures. The ability to see with spiritual eyes, to recognise God's unseen hand at work, sets the stage for miracles, provision, and real transformation. You do not ignore pain or difficulty, but you do not let circumstances dictate your vision or your voice. This is the posture Jesus modelled, speaking resurrection life even over what appeared hopeless or dead.

A kingdom mindset also taps into what can be called prophetic imagination. This is the God-given faculty that allows us to picture, from the heart, how God's purposes might unfold. It is disciplined, practical, and rooted in scriptural models, not fantasy, not wishful thinking. Prophetic imagination means training yourself to notice what God could do, not merely rehearsing possible disasters. For example, if a family is fractured by misunderstanding, someone operating in prophetic imagination will prayerfully recall stories of reconciliation like Joseph and his brothers, and begin to paint mental images of unity, forgiveness, and restoration. They do not simply "hope" for change they begin to imagine and pray toward a future shaped by God's promise, guided by biblical patterns of renewal. The Holy Spirit works in this process, ushering in fresh insight, creative solutions, and pathways forward that align with God's heart and character.

Mind His Business Not Theirs

Many people, even sincere Christians, struggle with a kind of spiritual near-sightedness. Modern culture, disappointment, and habit train us to focus only on what we can sense, manipulate, or measure. This can deaden spiritual sensitivity and keep our sight directed at visible problems, rather than the bigger picture. Doubt and cynicism crowd out the possibility of breakthrough, especially when the road has been hard. Some endlessly replay memories of failure or pain, while their gaze never rises to see how God remains at work beyond what is visible. To move beyond this, believers must become honest about their human tendencies toward tunnel vision and then intentionally shift their focus to God's overarching purposes. This is where renewing the mind comes alive: by repeatedly choosing to dwell on scripture, God's promises, and previous faithfulness, believers begin to see their life in a new light. Imagine, for instance, someone who feels trapped by financial limitations, yet day after day rehearses how God provided for the Israelites in the wilderness, or how Jesus fed five thousand with five loaf and two fish. Over time, the mindset bends toward expectation of provision rather than anxiety about lack.

Expanding spiritual vision requires daily habits that nurture faith. Here is a simple exercise to cultivate this kind of seeing:

- Set aside a regular time each day for focused prayer, specifically asking God to help you perceive His bigger purpose in your life's challenges.
- During prayer, ask the Holy Spirit to lift your eyes beyond present limitations. Focus on one area where you feel stuck, perhaps a strained relationship or financial uncertainty.
- Read aloud scriptures such as 2 Corinthians 4:18, anchoring your thoughts on eternal realities rather than fleeting circumstances.
- Pause to picture, with your mind's eye, what it would look like if God's promises came to life in your current situation. For example, if you envision reconciliation in a relationship, see yourself having an honest, healing conversation or imagine harmony being restored.
- Journal any emerging pictures, scriptures, or impressions, letting your heart speak freely.

- Over the week, revisit your entries to notice patterns, recurring scriptures, or inner nudges. This process helps you distinguish God's gentle direction from your own anxieties.

These steps might seem simple, but they require repeated, determined engagement. This is not mere optimism; it is the daily choice to interact with scripture, prayer, and the Holy Spirit's guidance. As you nurture this habit, fresh possibilities come into focus, and you prepare for breakthrough. The next section will equip you with practical, interactive exercises to break free from internal restrictions and turn spiritual vision into real-world momentum.

 ## Breaking Free from Limitations

Moving from the foundation of spiritual vision laid earlier in this chapter, now begin uncovering the beliefs that silently shape your actions. Scripture repeats the call to *"be transformed by the renewing of your mind,"* making it clear that inner renewal lies at the centre of kingdom living. To renew your mind, start with honest self-examination. Ask, what persistent doubts hold me back from pursuing God's promises? When do I find myself thinking, "That blessing is for others, not me," or "I shouldn't even try, I'm not enough"? These questions matter because unmasking limiting beliefs is the first step toward living in truth rather than fear. Take a journal or a blank page and write down the negative thoughts that echo in your heart. Capture the moments these doubts rise: Is it during prayer, while considering a new opportunity, or after making a mistake? Name them specifically, for example, "I am not equipped," "I will always fail," or "God's help is for people who have it all together." Honest recognition is not weakness; it is courage. When you identify these lies, you position yourself to replace them with the truth God declares over your life. Ask reflection questions such as:

- When do you feel God's promises do not apply to you?
- What fears hold you back from stepping into new opportunities?
- Which internal statements come up when you dream or plan for the future?
- Is there a recurring sense of unworthiness or condemnation?

If you write, "I don't have what it takes to lead," consider where that thought first took root. Was it a past failure, someone else's words, or simply a fear of disappointing God? Identifying the source enables you to address it with renewal and compassion rather than blame.

Armed with clarity about your personal barriers, prepare to wage war with truth. The next practice centres on crafting powerful, biblically anchored declarations. God created the world with His Word and calls His children to speak life aligned with His promises. Choose scripture as your foundation and personalise it with bold, present-tense language. If your limiting belief says, "I am weak," your declaration becomes,

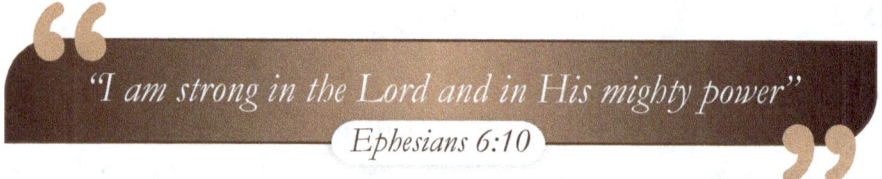

"I am strong in the Lord and in His mighty power"
Ephesians 6:10

If you feel unworthy, declare

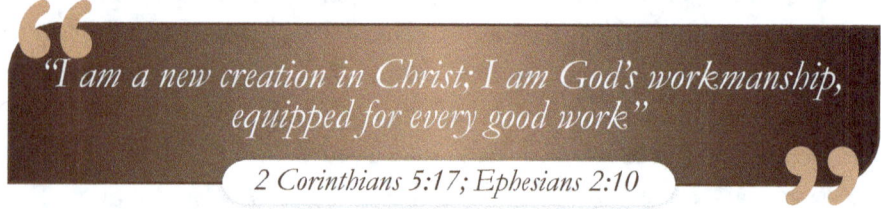

"I am a new creation in Christ; I am God's workmanship, equipped for every good work"
2 Corinthians 5:17; Ephesians 2:10

To compose your own:

- Identify a lie or limitation from your list.
- Find a scriptural promise or truth that counters it.
- Write your declaration in the first person, active, and positive language.
- State the declaration aloud daily, especially when old doubts surface.

Example 1: If your belief is, "I never get things right," write: "I have the mind of Christ. I am guided in wisdom and good judgment."

Example 2: For "God is distant from me," declare: "God is near to me; He will never leave nor forsake me."

This practice is not empty positive thinking. When you align your words with scripture, you declare the reality of God's kingdom over your own mind and circumstances (DuMont, 2023; Shawnpigg, 2024). Speak these truths boldly. Each word is an act of faith and a tool for transformation.

Transformation deepens through deliberate, practical action. Do not wait for perfect confidence before you move forward. Select one small but meaningful risk that challenges the limitation you identified. If fear tells you not to reach out for help, call someone you trust and ask for prayer. If you doubt your value, volunteer for a role that stretches your gifts. Taking this step is your way of saying, "I trust God's truth over my past experiences." In the process, repetition matters. The more you choose faith-inspired action in little ways, offering to pray for someone, speaking encouragement, sharing an idea, the easier courage becomes. Consistency turns isolated victories into a pattern of breakthrough.

Celebrate every stretch moment, no matter how minor it feels. Progress, not perfection, is the currency of lasting transformation. Record a moment of gratitude in your journal: "Today I made the call and didn't shrink back." Or share the story with a trusted friend, small group, or mentor who supports your journey. Vocalising victories builds confidence, honours God's work within you, and motivates continued effort even when setbacks occur. Do not let a step forward go unnoticed, celebration roots new identity and sustained momentum.

Continue to practice these exercises with persistence. Each time you confront a lie, speak truth, and act on it, you partner with God's transformative power. The next section will lead you further in developing the focused faith that strengthens this discipline, guiding you into unwavering confidence anchored wholly in Christ. Stay present in these tangible steps for now, your foundation is being laid.

 ## Developing Focused Faith

Faith never remains the same; it either grows through deliberate use or fades when neglected. Just as a muscle requires consistent exercise to gain strength, faith flourishes by steady engagement, each act of trust stretches its capacity and resilience. When someone meets a setback, a lost job, a closed door, a painful diagnosis, initial fear and doubt can overwhelm. But like an athlete pushing through resistance, a believer who responds with persistent trust in God's character develops a more robust, unwavering faith. It does not matter if the step is small, like choosing to pray in the morning despite anxiety, or large, such as forgiving an old wound. Each instance is an opportunity to flex spiritual muscle, reinforcing endurance for greater trials ahead

Challenges in life often present themselves as invitations to test and expand faith. Imagine the moment when an unexpected bill arrives, threatening to disrupt a family's finances. The natural instinct might be to worry or scramble for human solutions. However, viewing the situation as a faith exercise, a believer prays, seeks wise counsel, and intentionally remembers God's past faithfulness. These repeated acts transform a moment of stress into a moment of growth. Over time, such repeated choices lead to spiritual stamina and a deep-rooted security
that withstands future storms.

Growth in faith is more apparent when people intentionally recognise each step forward. Celebrating small wins like choosing gratitude, maintaining peace in a stressful meeting, or speaking kind words when annoyed, nurtures perseverance. Some journal their faithful decisions or share stories with trusted friends. As these minor victories gather, they create momentum, fuelling courage and hope for even more significant leaps of trust. Instead of focusing on failures or the size of remaining mountains, believers start seeing progress, which sparks motivation to persist.

Mind His Business Not Theirs

Real stories of faith bring this journey to life. The biblical account of Joshua leading the Israelites into the promised land offers a compelling picture of trust under pressure. When facing daunting walls and well-armed enemies, every step around Jericho required the choice to believe God's promise over visible reality. Scripture records God's encouragement to Joshua:

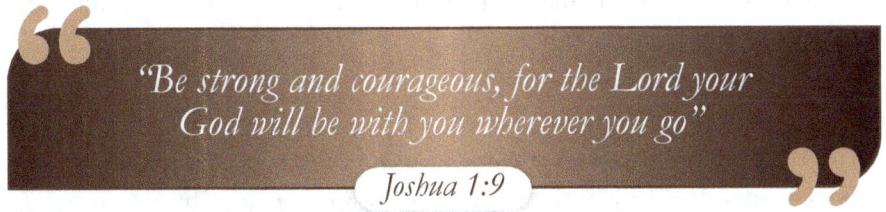

> "Be strong and courageous, for the Lord your God will be with you wherever you go"
>
> Joshua 1:9

The miracle did not come from wishful thinking but from action, obeying, marching, and praising even when the outcome was unclear. In the same way, contemporary testimonies echo these truths. Women and men navigating uncertainty, waiting for healing, searching for purpose, trusting God through relational pain, share how unwavering faith, tested by fire, guided them to breakthrough and peace. Their journeys teach that faithfulness is built by incremental steps: praying honestly, seeking encouragement in God's Word, making decisions aligned with conviction rather than convenience.

Expectant prayer stands out as a foundation for active, growing faith. This type of prayer involves coming to God with anticipation, not demanding a specific outcome but trusting fully that He responds according to His wisdom and love. Praying with expectation may look like starting each day by surrendering plans, inviting God to guide each step, and anchoring requests to promises found in scripture. Strategies include adopting a simple structure, for instance, the P.R.A.Y. rhythm: Praise, Repent, Ask, Yield, allowing space to affirm God's nature, confess fears, make requests, and submit to His will. Consistency matters. Setting a daily time for honest, focused prayer makes trust a reflex rather than a last resort.

Using a list of specific promises, such as

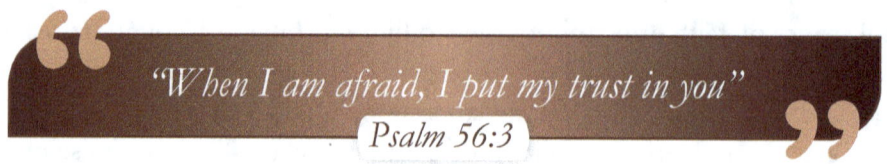

"When I am afraid, I put my trust in you"
Psalm 56:3

further anchors faith to unchanging truth, shifting attention from fluctuating circumstances to God's faithful character.

Doubt and negativity threaten to undermine resolve, often entering unnoticed through thoughts, conversations, or media. Developing spiritual alertness means discerning when a thought or influence distracts from faith. Replace anxious speculation with declarations of God's goodness and promises. Regularly read and meditate on scripture,
not merely for information but as fuel for conviction. Community matters too; surrounding oneself with friends and mentors who encourage trust, share testimony, and remind each other of God's works acts as a shield against despair. Structure moments of reflection, at the end of each day, recount victories, identify where faith grew, and ask
God for continued strength. This discipline creates spiritual clarity, develops habits that consistently reorient to hope, and cultivates a readiness to recognise and pursue
divine opportunity.

As minds grow accustomed to trusting God beyond visible circumstances, spiritual creativity awakens. Deep faith makes room for Holy Spirit-inspired ideas, unexpected solutions, and new ways to serve. In this renewed posture, imagination aligns not with fear but with kingdom possibility, paving the way for a vibrant, forward-looking life.

 **Imagination Sanctified**

The imagination is a divinely granted faculty that enables believers to preview God's possibilities before they materialise. Through scripture, God repeatedly invites His people to "see" with eyes of faith, whether it was Abraham counting stars to picture his descendants or the prophets envisioning a redeemed future. When imagination partners with the Holy Spirit, it becomes a canvas for divine inspiration and a source of creative solutions aligned with kingdom purposes. For example, someone seeking direction for their family consistently set aside time to pray, then allowed the Spirit to guide their imagination. As they pictured their children thriving and their relationships overflowing with grace, the vision prompted them to nurture those qualities daily, anchoring hope and fuelling specific prayers. By surrendering imagination, believers become available to receive God's inspired strategies and set their focus on purposes already in His heart.

Imagination, though, never exists in a vacuum. It is vulnerable to external messages, cultural narratives, and the residue of life's disappointments. When saturated by fear-driven thoughts, images of failure or inadequacy can take root, subtly reshaping expectations. For instance, a person repeatedly envisions rejection at work, even as they confess faith. These mental pictures can sabotage actions, reinforce self-doubt, and limit spiritual momentum, regardless of the truths declared verbally. Imaginations not intentionally guarded may become footholds for discouragement or temptation, particularly when unchecked scrolling, disturbing news cycles, or dwelling on past wounds populate the landscape of the mind. If the mind is left unrenewed, the creative faculty that is meant to partner with God instead projects worst-case scenarios, compounding anxiety and restricting the believer's openness to supernatural outcomes
(*Prayer Archives - Listening to God,* 2024).

Noticing this vulnerability is the precursor to change. Daily discipline is required to discern and redirect the course of imagination. One reliable exercise for sanctifying imagination involves several intentional steps. Begin by inviting the Holy Spirit with open-hearted prayer, specifically asking for awareness of any recurring mental images or narratives shaped by fear, regret, or worldly influence. For example, after such a prayer, an individual might realise they frequently picture themselves alone and unsupported, especially in uncertain seasons. Next, the person writes down the troubling image in detail, noting how it feels, when it tends to surface, and what triggers it.

After capturing the specific image, the seeker searches scripture for a clear, contradicting truth. If the recurring mental story is one of isolation, Hebrews 13:5 or Psalm 23 become anchor verses, reminding the believer of God's unwavering presence. Once the scripture is chosen, the next step is meditating on it with intention, reading it aloud, considering what it reveals about God's character, and letting its reality settle deep inside. The next actionable move is to deliberately replace the negative scenario with a new faith-filled mental picture that springs from the scripture's promise. For instance, the person might close their eyes and imagine walking through a valley with the Good Shepherd by their side, every need met, every fear answered in His presence. Sensory details, how the scene looks, what words God speaks, how peace feels, are included to make the vision vivid.

This mental replacement should be done daily, especially when old images intrude. Repetition is crucial because imagination is trained by exposure. Each time the mind tries to default to fear or past narratives, the believer returns to the scriptural vision, reinforcing truth and fostering an expectation that matches God's word. Someone struggling with financial worry, for example, could meditate on Philippians 4:19, repeatedly picturing God providing in concrete ways, groceries appearing, rent paid, children cared for, the specific outcomes promised by God. Every step in this practice builds on habits already introduced, such as faith declarations and verbal confession. Audibly declaring the scriptural truth right after meditating on it strengthens

the connection between thought, word, and expectation. Renewing the mind in this way, the believer cultivates a faith-filled lens through which all circumstances are interpreted, creating a mindset ripe
for divine intervention.

Imagination also becomes powerful in prayer, especially when actively employed to visualise God's promises as fulfilled realities. In a moment of intercession, the believer might picture a fractured relationship mended, seeing laughter, hearing forgiving words, and sensing the warmth of reconciliation. Someone praying for peace can imagine walking through their day unhurried and unaffected by stress, visualising inner calm as a lived reality. This prayerful use of imagination does not replace waiting on God, but anchors hope and strengthens endurance while answers unfold. By visualising outcomes soaked in God's promises, believers not only affirm expectation but also cooperate with the Spirit to expand their inner capacity for God's kingdom possibilities

 Bringing It All Together

Now that you understand how to renew your mind through God's truth, break free from limiting beliefs, and cultivate a focused faith anchored in scripture, you are equipped to see beyond natural barriers and embrace the greater purposes God has for your life. By consistently speaking His promises, taking small steps of faith, and aligning your imagination with the Holy Spirit, you can transform your thinking and open your spiritual eyes to new possibilities. This renewed mindset empowers you not only to overcome challenges but also to step boldly into God's kingdom work, confident that He is guiding and providing every step of the way. Keep practicing these disciplines daily, and watch as your faith grows stronger, your vision expands, and your life becomes a powerful testimony of transformation and hope.

KEY 5

PARTNERING WITH THE HOLY SPIRIT

*The Holy Spirit
does not just accompany you;
He amplifies what
Christ has put in you.*

Philip Dada Jr

Building a partnership with the Holy Spirit is the foundational key to walking in supernatural wisdom and faith, especially when it comes to the demanding arenas of business, career, ministry, and fulfilling your God-given purpose. This partnership begins and is sustained through the disciplined exercise of prayer, and among the most powerful expressions of that prayer is speaking in tongues. When you open yourself to pray in the Spirit, you are engaging in a divine exchange far beyond the limits of your natural understanding. This is the language of the Spirit, the groanings too deep for words that the Holy Spirit uses to intercede for you when you don't know how to pray as you ought (Romans 8:26-27).

This spiritual practice is not simply a ritual but a supernatural workout that strengthens and builds your faith in ways ordinary prayer cannot. Just as physical exercise conditions your body to endure and perform, praying in tongues conditions your spirit, invigorating it, renewing it, and aligning it more closely with God's heart. It becomes a channel of divine strength and wisdom, releasing power within you that propels you forward into boldness and clarity.

Faith built this way is unshakable because it is rooted in the unseen reality of God's kingdom, not limited by the fluctuations of your emotions or the uncertainties of your circumstances. It is a faith that stands firm amid storms, that hears God's whisper of peace when every external voice shout fear. This is the faith that moves mountains (Mark 11:23), the faith that inspires creativity, innovation, and resilience. It is the kind of faith that a wise master builder carries, someone who doesn't just plan projects or lead teams, but builds lasting legacies with eternal impact.

In the practical realm of business and career, this partnership with the Holy Spirit translates into supernatural wisdom. It enables you to discern the unseen currents in markets, to navigate complex relationships with grace, and to make decisions guided by divine insight rather than merely human logic. Proverbs 3:5-6 reminds us to "trust in the Lord with all our heart and lean not on our own understanding, but to acknowledge Him in all our ways so He can direct our paths."

Praying in tongues helps keep that trust alive and active. It creates a constant flow of communication with God that refines your vision and strengthens your strategic thinking.

In ministry and purpose-driven work, this connection is even more vital. The Holy Spirit empowers you to minister not just with words, but with authority and anointing that breaks chains and ushers healing. It is the Spirit's wisdom that leads you to speak life into situations, discern hearts, and build communities grounded in love and truth. The Spirit equips you as a master builder to construct not only physical projects but spiritual households, nurturing faith that endures and multiplies.

Many who have walked this path testify that praying in tongues expanded their capacity to handle pressure and responsibility. It creates a reservoir of spiritual strength from which you can draw when challenges arise. Psychologically, this kind of prayer promotes a deep inner peace, reducing anxiety and increasing mental clarity by releasing divine peace that transcends understanding (Philippians 4:7). It rewires the soul to respond with faith rather than fear, with wisdom rather than impulsiveness.

Imagine standing at the helm of your career or ministry, not relying solely on your own intellect or experience but partnered intimately with the Holy Spirit, who guides your every step. Every decision you make is infused with heavenly wisdom; every challenge faced with God-breathed courage. This is the heart of a master builder, one who constructs not just with hands but with Spirit-empowered vision and faith. As you continue to exercise yourself in prayer, especially in the gift of tongues, your partnership with the Holy Spirit grows stronger. Your spiritual muscles develop, your faith deepens, and your wisdom becomes sharper. You become a conduit for God's power to build His kingdom on earth, in your workplace, your family, your community, and beyond. This is not a calling reserved for a select few. It is an invitation for every believer to step into their destiny, empowered by the Spirit, anchored in faith, and equipped with wisdom to build well. So, embrace this discipline with open hands and heart, knowing that as you do, you are being formed into a wise master builder, capable of erecting lasting, kingdom-impacting structures that glorify God and bless generations to come.

Mind His Business Not Theirs

The entire story of building my fashion brand, Philip Dada Jr (PDJ) is rooted in one truth: it has been a journey of partnership with the Holy Ghost. From the very beginning, I knew that if this brand was to carry weight, it could not be built solely on business principles, marketing tactics, or human effort. It had to be carried by the Spirit of Life. There were seasons where I would go into fasting and prayer, not simply asking God to bless what I was doing but waiting to hear what He was saying. And in those times, He would whisper, sometimes it was an idea for a product, other times a strategy for expansion, and occasionally, He would tell me to simply hold back and wait.

I've learned that those whispers are not suggestions, they are instructions that carry life. Every time I have obeyed, I've seen results that no amount of planning could manufacture. I remember moments when, just after prayer and obedience, major celebrities would suddenly purchase one of our suits or kaftans, opening doors to circles I could not have reached on my own. I've seen brand activations succeed beyond imagination, not because we had the largest budget or the biggest team, but because the Spirit had gone ahead of us. Even in the quieter moments, when He instructed me to wait rather than move, I later realised He was positioning the brand for greater impact.

PDJ is not just a fashion house; it is living proof of what happens when entrepreneurship is stewarded as a spiritual assignment. The same Spirit who hovered over the waters in Genesis is the One who breathes creativity, excellence, and strategy into this brand today. And what I have come to understand deeply is this: success in kingdom entrepreneurship does not come from striving, but from partnership. When you build with the Holy Ghost, you are not reacting to trends, you are responding to heaven. That is why I can speak with authority: everything you see in PDJ today is not just the result of hard work, but the fruit of walking step by step with the Spirit of God.

The challenge of living out faith in environments where spiritual values are overlooked or even questioned, is a reality many believers face daily. Whether in bustling offices, competitive industries, or diverse cultural settings, the tension between personal conviction and external expectations can create moments of isolation, pressure, and unanswered questions.

Mind His Business Not Theirs

Yet beneath this struggle lies an invitation to something deeper: a partnership with the Holy Spirit that sustains integrity, guides decisions, and shapes character in ways that often go unseen but have lasting impact.

This chapter invites readers to explore how walking closely with the Holy Spirit equips believers to respond faithfully within secular spaces. It offers practical perspectives on enduring challenges without compromise, influencing others through quiet, consistent excellence, navigating complex ethical situations with divine wisdom, and recognising the subtle victories that come from Spirit-led living. By learning to discern the Spirit's guidance and aligning motives with God's purposes, individuals can cultivate a resilient and effective witness that honours Christ in every aspect of their professional and personal lives.

Partnering with the Holy Spirit in Hostile Environments

In professional settings that rarely acknowledge Christian values, subtle but profound influence often flows from the Holy Spirit's presence within a believer. Unlike external displays, this invisible influence expresses itself through unwavering honesty, patience under pressure, and acts of humility or kindness. When a believer chooses integrity, refusing to falsify numbers even when the team expects it or refusing to join in slanderous conversations about a peer, the Spirit quietly uses that action to set a different tone. It is not dramatic, nor does it draw immediate attention, but the ripple effect of one person's righteousness can nudge the conscience of a workplace. Sometimes a simple act, such as refusing to gossip, sparks curiosity in others, opening the door for deeper spiritual conversations later, even if resistance or indifference initially prevails.

Invisible Influence Through Character

The Holy Spirit specialises in working through what outsiders consider ordinary character traits, truthfulness, gentleness, steadfastness, but these attributes become channels for divine power. Believers may find themselves dealing with disrespect or facing pressure to compromise.

Instead of matching resentment with resentment, responding with grace demonstrates the transformative presence within. For example, an employee unfairly blamed for a failed project listens patiently, avoids retaliation, and seeks resolution with humility. Even if others remain unmoved, these unseen responses plant seeds that God alone can water and bring to fruition. Over time, colleagues notice a distinct steadiness, even if they cannot name its source.

 ## Standing Alone With God

Isolation may mark the path of those who stand firm for Christ in places unfriendly to faith. Rejection or exclusion often comes, whether through missed promotions, subtle mockery, or feeling out of step with prevailing values. In such moments, the Holy Spirit becomes a vital companion, offering more than mere comfort. Regular prayer, meditation on scripture, and privately pouring out frustrations replenish spiritual courage. After enduring a belittling meeting, a believer may retreat briefly to their car, pray for their antagonists, and ask the Spirit for wisdom on how to proceed. Often in those quiet, overlooked moments, God imparts unexpected insight or assurance. The believer may receive clarity for a challenging task or sense a joyful confidence that transcends circumstance. The Spirit's ministry in private sustains resilience in public, replacing isolation with a sense of belonging to God.

 ## Quiet Consistency

In environments demanding proof of results, the Spirit leads not through showmanship but through steady, authentic perseverance. Quiet consistency is a powerful testimony. Resisting shortcuts in reporting, faithfully following procedures, and performing mundane responsibilities as if working for God, rather than human supervisors, draw on scriptures such as Colossians 3:23. Consider a manager who never misrepresents sales numbers and always treats support staff respectfully, year after year, even if no one commends them. Over time, this endurance forms a reputation for trustworthiness and excellence, gradually drawing the respect of both colleagues and superiors.

The Holy Spirit amplifies these steady choices, which often go unnoticed, weaving them into a silent network of influence that shapes the culture of an organisation or team. Even when promotions are passed over, or results seem absent, the unshakable integrity wrought by the Spirit becomes a beacon, proving impossible to ignore forever.

 Purpose in Adversity

Adversity, whether in the form of conflict, job loss, or crises at work, often serves as a divinely orchestrated opportunity. The Spirit uses such seasons to refine commitment, redirect calling, or deepen dependence. Suppose a professional is pressured to act unethically, refuses, and is dismissed as a result. Far from defeat, this loss can lead through the Spirit's leading to a position where their ethical standards are valued, or open doors to a calling that aligns more closely with God's purposes. In another scenario, sustained tension with a supervisor might become the catalyst for growth in patience, creativity, or boldness through reliance on the Spirit's prompting. A Spirit-filled posture asks, "Holy Spirit, what are You doing in this?" and chooses faith-filled, practical steps instead of retreating into complaint or bitterness.

Progressively, these elements, subtle influence, standing alone, quiet consistency, and transformation in hardship, compose a way of life. Faithful witness, often unseen, builds trust over time and establishes credibility. A workplace marked by even one Spirit-filled believer gradually shifts as integrity and excellence become visible. This enduring witness, coupled with the Spirit's wisdom and strength, lays the foundation for a life that attracts attention not through loud declarations, but through reliable fruit. Such lives invite questions, draw others near, and open broader avenues for leadership and influence fuelled by the Spirit's quiet power.

Demonstrating Spirit-Empowered Excellence as Witness

Quiet influence over time grows roots that others notice, even when its source is not shouted aloud. In fast-paced offices, creative studios, and healthcare corridors, the steady hand of someone guided by the Holy Spirit often stands apart without fanfare. Early mornings, deadlines, misunderstandings, across all these moments, a Spirit-empowered consistency builds a kind of trust that outlasts applause. Reliability and perseverance under pressure send ripples through teams and projects. These qualities begin as internal choices, shaped in silence, but they eventually create visible results that invite curiosity.

Excellence led by the Spirit differs from striving for personal achievement. It resists shortcuts and does not measure success in comparison with others. Instead, each task becomes a chance to serve through diligence and wisdom borrowed from God. In business meetings, classrooms, or hospital rotations, employees and leaders directed by the Spirit often solve problems with an unusual calm or deliver on difficult assignments with integrity that runs deeper than company policy. These acts tend to speak on their own long before the workers do.

 ## Spirit-led Fruitfulness that Glorifies Jesus

True fruitfulness means more than just impressive numbers or financial results. The Spirit's work produces lasting and meaningful change, solutions that endure, cultures that heal, and teams that function with surprising unity. For believers, this fruit often blooms under the surface before it springs into sight. Consider an engineer known for gracefully handling stressful deadlines and delivering work that always exceeds the norm. Coworkers soon start asking how she keeps her peace or solves challenges that leave others frazzled. Instead of turning these questions into a stage for self-celebration, she points out how prayer or wisdom from above helps her. This reply opens new layers in the relationship, making space for deeper talks about faith and life.

In another example, a small business owner refuses to cut corners to increase profits, even when no one would ever notice. Over time, clients and employees realise they can trust him. His faithful decisions, day after day, build a reputation for fairness that attracts loyal business, and eventually, people come seeking advice or even asking about his values. Rather than using these moments for self-promotion, he gives credit to God as the source of his standards. A sincere comment like, "I try to honour God in my decisions and trust Him with the outcome," intrigues rather than intimidates. Opportunities for influence become everyday moments rather than staged presentations.

 Earning Influence Through Dependability

Lasting influence rarely comes in a single, attention-grabbing moment. Leaders and professionals who remain steady and dependable especially under strain are the ones colleagues trust for hard projects, honest feedback, or confidential advice. The quieter the environment regarding faith, the greater the power of this credibility. When others see that a believer's excellence does not depend on oversight or chasing kudos, they begin to wonder about the cause beneath it all.

These bridges are built not just with skill but with a Spirit that is approachable and real. When a team member notices your approach and says, "You always seem to know what to do," a proud answer closes the conversation, but gratitude opens a door. A simple, genuine response, "God really helps me", is more powerful than a rehearsed speech. Over time, this humble approach gives space for honest questions. It removes pressure and brings conversations about faith into ordinary life.

Humility that Keeps Hearts Open

Humility remains the constant companion of true excellence. The Holy Spirit not only empowers results but also shapes the attitude behind them. He gently checks even the finest hint of self-congratulation. Spiritual pride, even in subtle forms like broadcasting how prayer led to success or using faith as a badge, raises silent walls. People sense when credit rings untrue or when achievements are packaged as humble brags.

Authentic humility keeps hearts soft and relationships healthy. When others give praise, believers can redirect it to God without clichés or sanctimonious tone. Instead of saying, "All glory to God," in a way that ends the discussion, a believer can say, "I really need God's help each day," or "I wouldn't have managed this without His guidance." These remarks encourage curiosity and invite further conversation while keeping the focus on the ultimate source of strength.

Spirit led excellence often raises questions about motive. As believers experience greater trust and influence, it becomes necessary to examine the aims behind their pursuit. Such honest examination allows space for the Holy Spirit to uncover hidden ambitions, purify intentions and align desire with God's glory not self-seeking. This heart work forms the foundation for lasting service that both excels and remains humble, allowing God's light to shine through every accomplishment

 ## Keeping Motives Sacred Amid Secular Success

Spirit-empowered excellence goes beyond personal achievement or admiration. It quietly turns attention from self to Christ, even in environments where faith is met with scepticism or resistance. When believers dedicate themselves to high standards, showing skilfulness, dependability, and compassion, the result is often curiosity. Colleagues and clients may wonder about the source of this unusual integrity and strength. But real faithfulness is not a performance act or a branding choice. The Holy Spirit guards against the subtle temptation to use success as a stage for personal glory rather than as an invitation into God's story. How easy it is to desire excellence for applause, promotions, or security, all the while missing the deeper purpose of kingdom influence.

The difference between excellence that draws others to Christ and excellence that circles back to self, lies in the motives that drive each decision, pursuit, or risk. These hidden motives shape the sustainability, fruitfulness, and impact of any accomplishment. Sometimes even believers are not fully aware of what fuels their ambition. The Holy Spirit alone can search out these inner areas and bring hidden motives to light. Achievements that begin with pure, God-centred motives tend to multiply peace, stamina, and joy even in challenging seasons. Ambition driven by insecurity, pride, or comparison, on the other hand, eventually unravels. It leaves burnout, dissatisfaction, or conflict in its wake because it seeks validation rather than service.

Consider a manager in a competitive organisation who is suddenly offered a promotion. The opportunity is prestigious, the salary substantial. Yet as she contemplates accepting, she finds herself wrestling with a quiet unease, the question surfaces: "Is this move about stewarding my gifts for God's purposes or simply securing greater influence and recognition?" The Holy Spirit often meets believers in these quiet moments. He gently surfaces pride that pretends to be vision, exposes the fear of missing out that masquerades as diligent ambition, and invites honest prayers for guidance. When given space, the Spirit encourages words like those of Psalm 139: "Search me, O God, and know my heart…See if there is any offensive way in me." In those moments, the pursuit of success is reshaped. It is no longer about climbing ladders. It becomes about representing Christ faithfully, regardless of the title.

Another example is the entrepreneur whose company begins to flourish after years of struggle. Praise pours in, awards, media attention, industry recognition. Amid the celebration, he senses the Spirit quietly prompting him to ask, "Who gets the credit here? Have I surrendered this venture, or am I fuelling my own legacy?" Sincere answers are rarely comfortable. The Spirit's role is not to shame, but to cleanse, to prune, to realign. Sometimes this leads to specific acts of surrender: giving away a bonus to serve those in need, mentoring younger colleagues without fanfare, or crediting the team for what only God could have orchestrated. These responses, shaped by Spirit-guided evaluation, seal a believer's influence and keep the heart free from the corrosion of ego.

Unchecked ambition produces exhaustion and fleeting impact because it runs on willpower rather than grace. Leaders who refuse regular heart checks are vulnerable to anxiety when results waver, defensiveness if ever criticised, and shallow influence if priorities shift from God to self. Lasting impact, on the other hand, is possible only when ambition is continually placed before God for refining. The altar is where vision is purified, where God prunes what serves only self, reshapes what can glorify Him, and multiplies what is surrendered completely. When dreams are consecrated, opportunity widens in unexpected ways. A believer may be entrusted with greater visibility, but now the spotlight does not blind, it reveals Christ. Wisdom grows, and authority is exercised with humility.

External achievement and internal holiness are not enemies, but the second sustains the first. The world applauds results, but scripture measures fruit by character and obedience. The Holy Spirit teaches that sustainable success comes from a heart kept soft and honest before God. Election to a council, the launch of a thriving business, or the approval of a difficult client, these victories are safely handled when the inner life is marked by frequent, Spirit-led examination. The applause fades, yet a life lived with clean motives yields peace, resilience, and influence that shape others for generations.

In secular or ambiguous settings, where ethical boundaries blur and motivations are easily disguised, this kind of Spirit-led self-awareness becomes a shield and a compass. Discernment grows in those who regularly invite the Spirit to test their ambitions. Spiritual attentiveness safeguards integrity and shapes responses, especially when difficult choices threaten to erode one's sense of right and wrong. In such environments, a believer's inner alignment with the Spirit proves essential, not only for personal peace but for lasting witness.

Navigating Ethical Dilemmas with the Spirit's Guidance

Each day at work or in the marketplace, believers encounter situations that aren't neatly covered by the rulebook or corporate code of conduct. Sometimes a colleague presents a shortcut that saves money but skirts transparency. A client might request a quiet omission in a report that twists the truth but keeps a contract secure. In moments like these, the Holy Spirit serves as our internal compass, His presence pressing in to signal discomfort, unease, or a pricking of conscience. Rather than ignoring this sense or pushing past it, the disciplined disciple learns to pause, even if for only a breath. When inner tension rises in a budget meeting or when signing off on that presentation, quietly pray, "Holy Spirit, is this right?" This silent invitation may bring a sudden sense of clarity, a warning, or a deepened peace that steadies your resolve. An operations manager, for example, may be presented with an inflated invoice to approve. In that moment, a tightening in her spirit signals danger. By pausing and calling on the Spirit for wisdom, she presses for transparency rather than passing it along. Though it may spark tension, the unseen assurance of God's peace fortifies her against inner compromise.

Recognising the complexity of these situations, rely on a daily practice of asking the Spirit for renewed discernment before you step into the doors of your workplace, boardroom, or virtual call. Begin your morning asking, "Lord, show me what's beneath the surface today. Make me sensitive to what honours You." This anticipation sets a posture of heightened spiritual awareness. Picture a team leader who has sensed that his company is sweeping underperformance under the rug prior to a board review. By inviting the Holy Ghost's insight, he discerns not only the facts but also the subtle motivations and fears playing out among his team. As each new situation arises, he practices moment-by-moment dialogue with the Spirit, never assuming that past solutions automatically apply. This constant communion develops spiritual reflexes, so that ultimately, God's values, not pressure, reputation, or convenience, shape each response.

Mind His Business Not Theirs

Drawing ethical lines in ambiguous territory is not just about mental determination but about inviting the Holy Spirit to illuminate and confirm where boundaries belong. Take time to write out a personal boundary statement whenever faced with recurring pressure, a type of line in the sand. This might sound like, "I will not sign off on financial statements that disguise our liabilities, regardless of pressure from above." Pray over this statement, asking the Spirit for clarity and courage, then keep it visible, a phone note, a desk card, a tucked-away reminder. When temptation arises or when higher-ups insist that everyone 'does it this way,' revisit this boundary. The Spirit strengthens resolve through the act of remembering; inner conviction transforms from fleeting feeling to settled line, guarded by supernatural help even when your stance is met with confusion or suspicion.

Sometimes, the Spirit's empowerment shows itself most in when, and how, you speak up or remain silent. Suppose during an interdepartmental project meeting, gossip starts circling about a staff member's private issues. The urge to confront or withdraw may battle within. The Spirit may nudge you to offer a short, redirecting word, "Let's focus on the task", or may prompt silent intercessory prayer for those involved, holding you back from words that come from frustration or self-righteousness. This posture of listening for the Spirit's promptings rather than reacting impulsively is what separates self-confidence from Spirit-led courage. When the Spirit gives peace to speak the truth in a proposal meeting, or restraint to hold back when others press you for an answer, recognise that His timing and tone are crucial. Speaking with the Holy Spirit's help often means delivering words that are both clear and merciful, so that your integrity never masquerades as pride.

Every step of this renewed partnership draws a thin but unbreakable line between outward reputation and inward Christlikeness. It is not perfection, but daily obedience, sometimes visible only to God, which becomes the truest mark of Spirit-living in contested spaces. Each act of yielding, pausing for wisdom, drawing new boundaries, courageously speaking or holding silent, plants seeds that God will honour. These practices help you remain unshaken when others take shortcuts. Soon, small, Spirit-backed moments of impact will become clear reminders of grace at work, preparing you to recognise and celebrate God's faithfulness ahead.

Celebrating Spirit-Led Victories in Secular Life

One sign of mature partnership with the Holy Ghost is learning to notice subtle victories in settings where God's presence is not always acknowledged. As the believer grows in discernment and purity of motive, the Spirit begins to spotlight moments of breakthrough that may appear ordinary at first glance. An atmosphere of tension at work starts to shift after intentional prayer for peace. In a project meeting marked by competing interests, you feel calm patience where you once braced for conflict. The Holy Ghost draws attention to these events, showing that divine intervention is not reserved for dramatic miracles but is woven through daily life. Thanking Him right away for these wins preserves a spiritual perspective, maintains humility, and renews vitality for future obedience.

People occasionally overlook the significance of a kept peace or a gentle response, assuming that spiritual victories must be large or public. Yet the Holy Ghost specialises in shaping character and outcomes in quiet ways. For example, a professional who has endured months of negativity develops a sudden burden to pray over their environment. Over time, the group dynamic noticeably softens, harmony returns, and discouragement lifts. Remembering to thank the Spirit for these changes transforms thankfulness into a regular posture, strengthening trust in His continual presence and activity.

 ### Spirit-Journaling: A Self-Help Exercise

Keeping track of Spirit-led wins forms a powerful habit that reinforces faith and senses God's faithfulness in real time. A Spirit-journal does not need to be elaborate. Its value comes from the simple act of recording moments where divine help was evident. Here's a straightforward method:

1. Set aside a quiet moment at the end of each day or week.
2. Ask the Holy Ghost to help you recall breakthroughs, answered prayers, or moments of clarity.
3. Write a few lines about each event. Summarise what happened, the prayer or need that preceded it, and any insights gained.
4. Include specific details, names, dates, emotions, and outcomes, to make each entry memorable.
5. Review the journal during seasons of discouragement or dryness, recalling God's track record of faithfulness.

For example, an entrepreneur may document an unexpected solution to a technical problem after asking the Spirit for guidance. Or a manager might record a significant conversation with a team member, noting a sense of unity restored after prayer. Over time, the journal becomes a living testimony, grounding confidence in fresh remembrance rather than vague nostalgia.

 ### Wise and Spirit-Led Testimony in Secular Spaces

Sharing breakthroughs in secular or mixed environments demands discernment and tact. In professional or diverse settings, unfiltered or overly spiritual language can invite resistance instead of hope. The Holy Ghost counsels on what to say, when to pause, and when to hold victories quietly before God. This practice honours both the dignity of listeners and the sacredness of your experience.

For example, a business leader might explain a season of team harmony as the result of intentional listening and kindness, mentioning prayer for wisdom only if the conversation allows. Sometimes, the Spirit signals to wait before sharing deeper details, preserving the moment until a more open door appears. Spirit-led sharing involves a careful listening posture, both to God and to those around you, ensuring that conversations remain safe and constructive.

Mind His Business Not Theirs

 Step-by-Step Exercise for Spirit-Led Testimony

Sharing breakthroughs in secular or mixed environments demands discern

- Take a deep breath and pause before speaking about a breakthrough.
- Silently ask the Holy Ghost for guidance regarding content, timing, and words.
- Assess the atmosphere and openness of your audience.
- Only proceed if you sense inner peace and clarity to share.
- Adjust your wording to make sense to those unfamiliar with spiritual language.
- If the setting is not right, hold the testimony quietly before God or pray for a future opportunity.

Imagine you receive a job promotion after a long season of hard work, prayer, and perseverance. In a meeting, you describe it as the result of dedicated effort and wisdom. If led, you briefly mention having sought insight through prayer, just enough to spark curiosity, not defensiveness.

 Ongoing Encouragement and Celebration

Gathering with the Holy Spirit in gratitude provides consistent strength for the journey ahead. Scheduling a weekly "thanksgiving appointment" with God can anchor this discipline. Take ten quiet minutes to review the week for moments big or small, where the Spirit's touch was evident. Pause after each recollection and offer thanks, acknowledging even simple provisions, reconciliations, or peaceful days. Through this routine, celebration becomes a source of renewed joy, deepening your resolve to keep walking with the Spirit when challenges arise. This rhythm infuses professional and personal life with durable confidence that each step, each win, and each testimony is guided by a living, ever-present Holy Ghost.

Concluding Thoughts

Now that we understand how the Holy Spirit empowers believers to live with integrity, discernment, and humility in challenging secular environments, we can move forward with confidence to embody this Spirit-led partnership daily. By embracing quiet influence through character, standing firm amid opposition, navigating ethical complexities with wisdom, and celebrating subtle victories, we build a foundation for lasting impact that honours God beyond applause or recognition. This ongoing journey calls us to remain vigilant in examining our motives, attentive to the Spirit's guidance, and faithful in small acts of obedience, knowing that these shape not only our own hearts but also the cultures around us. As we step into workplaces, marketplaces, and leadership roles renewed by the Spirit's power, we become living testimonies of Christ's presence, inviting others to glimpse His transforming love through our steady faithfulness and purposeful excellence.

KEY 6

EXCELLING
GET THE WORK DONE!

The day yields its treasures to those who act; delay leaves only the bitter taste of what might have been.

Philip Dada Jr

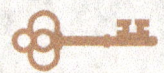

I remember one early morning in 2021 when I was fully consumed with the burden of building the tailoring factory for PDJ in Nigeria. Deep inside, I sensed that if I did not move with urgency at that moment, I would miss a divine window of opportunity. I knew I was going to get married the following year and relocate to London, and so all that was in my mind was a single thought: I must get it done. There was no time for delay, no time for procrastination. I was convinced that God had graced me specifically for that season, and that His hand was upon me to accomplish the assignment. That morning, as I was heading out to work with determination written all over me, my mum looked at me and in Hausa said, **"duba yadda yake tafiya kamar tsunami"** which means "look at how he is moving like a tsunami." My siblings laughed so hard when she said it, and I laughed too, but the truth is, it was the perfect description of my mindset at that time. I was like a storm in motion, determined to accomplish what God had placed before me.

That season taught me something powerful that has never left me. The mission of God on your life requires urgency. It is not enough to know His will, it is not enough to talk about His will, and it is not even enough to admire His will. You must do it. There are too many people who love the idea of hearing God, who enjoy the revelation and the spiritual high of knowing His plans, but when it comes to execution, they fall short. If you truly understand that the grace of God is upon you for an assignment, then your response must be action. My mindset then and still now is shaped by this: when God speaks and when He opens a window, you move like a tsunami. You obey fully, you obey quickly, and you obey with force. That is how destiny advances.

"Excellence is doing ordinary things extraordinarily well," a mentor once told me. Yet, when faced with the daily demands of work, leadership, and service, it can feel nearly impossible to sustain such a high standard. Tasks grow repetitive, motivation fades, and the call to wholehearted effort becomes obscured by distraction or fatigue. Many struggle between the temptation to settle for average, and the desire to honour God with their talents and time.

This tension reveals a deeper truth: excellence transcends natural ability or discipline alone. It begins where human effort meets spiritual dependence, inviting the Holy Spirit to empower every action and decision. This chapter explores how believers can move beyond passivity and procrastination, embracing practical habits and divine partnership that transform ordinary work into worship. It offers guidance on cultivating resilience in adversity, activating gifts for kingdom impact, and using modern tools to steward time and talents wisely. The goal is clear, getting the work done with faithfulness, vigour, and a legacy rooted in God's purposes.

Spirit-Empowered Excellence & Work as Worship

In the grind of professional obligations, church leadership, or even chores at home, a pattern can settle in, one where tasks become routine, effort flattens out, and the horizon of possibility shrinks to meet ordinary expectation. Scripture calls for something altogether different. When believers pursue excellence, not through sheer will or natural talent, but through surrender to the Holy Spirit, everyday work takes on an eternal significance. Daniel, surrounded by adversaries in Babylon, rose to unimagined influence because "an excellent spirit was in him" and his wisdom pointed to a source beyond the ordinary. When Joseph, betrayed and forgotten in Egypt, continued to serve and interpret with faithfulness and humility, God's favour thrust him into pivotal leadership "because the Lord was with Joseph and gave him success." Their outer achievements always rested on a
deeper spiritual foundation.

What set Daniel and Joseph apart was not only their competence but the clear evidence of God's empowering presence in their routines. Their insight and resilience were spiritual in origin, not products of mere self-reliance. For believers today, excellence begins where pride ends and collaboration with the Holy Spirit starts. Zechariah 4:6 offers the living foundation, *"Not by might, nor by power, but by my Spirit, says the Lord of hosts."* This refocuses ambition: productivity alone does not carry kingdom impact unless it arises from Spirit-led dependence.

Mind His Business Not Theirs

Daily labour, whether strategic meetings or unseen household tasks, holds the potential to become an act of worship. Colossians 3:23 reveals the heart of sacred excellence: *"Whatever you do, work at it with all your heart, as working for the Lord, not for men."* The smallest duties offered to God become valuable. This understanding equips Christians to reject mediocrity, not out of anxiety, but from bold assurance that their assignments no matter how small or secular, have eternal weight.

One critical shift is learning to invite the Holy Spirit into every aspect of work. This is not limited to "church work" or overt ministry. Daniel's excellence shone in a pagan court; Joseph influenced a godless system. The anointing of the Spirit is meant for believers wherever God has placed them, in secular or sacred context. This perspective brings spiritual fire to professional and personal diligence, enabling supernatural results and new levels of wisdom, creativity, and perseverance.

Paul's testimony amplifies this paradox: God's strength reaches its fullest expression when believers bring their sharpest weaknesses and limitations into honest surrender (2 Corinthians 12:9). In work, admitting inadequacy opens the way for an abundance that could not have been manufactured by talent alone. When self-effort loses its grip, prayerful dependence and openness to divine help leads to insight, solutions, and inner stamina that defy natural explanation.

 Inviting the Holy Spirit into Your Workday

Excellence often hinges on the small, secret choices made throughout each day. A habit of sanctifying work by prayer strengthens a sustained partnership with the Spirit.

- Before beginning your main daily tasks, pause and invite the Holy Spirit to be present and to guide your decisions and actions.
- Surrender the work ahead of you to God, naming specific projects or meetings, and ask for God's wisdom, creativity, and favour.

- As you work, remain attentive to inner nudges or fresh ideas that may come from the Spirit. Trust these prompts, especially when faced with obstacles or routine responsibility.
- At moments of stress or fatigue, pray for God's strength and endurance, thanking Him for His presence and power at work in your weakness.
- Conclude tasks by thanking God and asking Him to use your efforts and faithfulness for His greater purposes.

Consider Brooke, a manager at a community organisation. Each morning, she sets aside five minutes at her desk to dedicate her day to God. She prays over her schedule, staff interactions, and current projects, deliberately surrendering both her expertise and anxieties. As challenges arise, an urgent deadline, a difficult conversation, Brooke chooses not to strive alone. Instead, she draws on the Spirit's guidance, noticing fresh approaches and unexpected favour. By day's end, she reviews her work with gratitude, confident that even her most mundane efforts have become meaningful service to Christ.

This pattern grounds labour firmly in the sacred. Practical discipline and deep spiritual reliance unite, transforming jobs, chores, and leadership roles into channels for God's goodness and power. Faithfulness and integrity gain new urgency and joy. Serving others acquires lasting value, echoing Jesus' words that "whatever you did for one of the least…you did for me." As believers cultivate these practices, work ceases to be ordinary. Sanctified, it becomes worship. The same Spirit who empowers above-average results will also ignite hidden gifts and sustain resilience, further expanding what God can do through a surrendered life.

Multiplying Talents & Resilience in Adversity

Each believer carries God-given potential that the world urgently needs. Scripture confirms this in 1 Peter 4:10, which calls all Christians to use the gifts they have received to serve others as faithful stewards of God's grace. Too often, these gifts remain dormant. Spiritual gifts lie undiscovered. Natural talents, like communication, teaching, or creativity, are dismissed as "common sense" or "nothing special." Yet, God delights in using the ordinary for extraordinary impact.

Stepping into excellence means a rigorous self-awareness, honestly searching out what He has planted within.

A clear path toward this discovery blends biblical faith with practical assessment. Begin with prayerful openness, inviting the Holy Spirit to shine light on strengths you may overlook. Adding a short spiritual gifts test, or reviewing recent successes in business or ministry, can yield surprising results. Seek input from trusted mentors, friends, or colleagues. Their encouragements often point out recurring traits, perhaps your instinct to comfort, your knack for strategic thinking, or the calm you bring under pressure.

Distinguishing between natural and spiritual gifts brings greater clarity for action. Natural gifts can include organising projects, articulating vision, or crafting creative solutions. Spiritual gifts, such as discernment, faith, or leadership, show up in supernatural moments like sensing God's direction during an important decision or exhorting someone at just the right time. For instance, imagine an executive who manages teams with excellence (natural gift: leadership) but also frequently offers God-inspired wisdom when conflicts arise (spiritual gift: discernment). These layers, woven together, amplify kingdom influence in any environment.

A vibrant spiritual life centres on prayerful reflection. Allow space for God to highlight strengths, renew vision, or gently challenge excuses. He illuminates what might seem hidden or unimportant. In the words of James 1:5, *"any who lack wisdom can ask God, who gives generously without reproach."* Through this ongoing dialogue, even ordinary work becomes sacred ground for discovery and growth.

Faithfulness with these gifts requires courageous obedience, not just passive awareness. The parable of the talents powerfully illustrates this principle. Three servants receive resources based on their capacity. Two invest and multiply, the third hides his out of fear. Jesus rebukes inaction, not small beginnings. The invitation is not to wait for rare "big moments," but to offer whatever gifts you have, wherever you are.

Volunteering to mentor a colleague, running a small-group Bible study, or launching a faith-based business all qualify as kingdom building. Great influence starts by moving forward in faith, trusting God to magnify outcomes.

 Gift Activation Audit

- Reflect in prayer and ask God for fresh insight into both your natural and spiritual gifts.
- List all your talents, strengths, and skills. Use feedback from others to identify areas you might miss.
- Pinpoint two skills or gifts you have underutilised or neglected.
- Commit to a tangible action this week using these gifts, such as teaching a class, building a resource, joining a ministry, or innovating at your workplace.
- Journal the results, recording breakthroughs, lessons, or encouragements received from others.

Excellence grows as gifts are sharpened and stewarded daily. This does not happen by accident. Continual learning through in-depth books, online classes, podcasts, or regular mentorship, polishes both natural and spiritual skills. Modern tools can help shape the process. Digital journals allow you to track personal growth, log meaningful feedback, or set weekly goals. AI productivity apps schedule time for skill-building, turning intention into habit. One Christian entrepreneur enrolled in a negotiation course, tracked progress in a daily journal, and reflected on spiritual lessons alongside business skills. Within months, he found greater influence in contracts and a deepened connection to those he served.

Even the most gifted leader faces adversity. Seasons of discouragement or injustice are unavoidable. What distinguishes a spirit of excellence is grit, the choice to press forward, motivated not by self-will but by anchored hope. Joseph's life testifies to the fruit of sustained diligence under pressure. Betrayed and falsely accused, he honoured God with unwavering integrity, right where he was.

When setbacks threaten, scriptural truths serve as anchors. Romans 5:3-5 promises that suffering produces perseverance, persistence shapes character, and character fuels hope that does not disappoint.

 Spiritual Endurance Toolkit

- Choose a passage of scripture that speaks to perseverance (such as Romans 5:3-5 or 2 Corinthians 4:17).
- Each morning, read and pray over this verse, asking God for perspective and hope.
- When facing setbacks, pause to journal the experience, noting emotions, thoughts, and prayers.
- After journaling, write one practical adjustment you can make, such as seeking counsel, changing approach, or intentionally serving others amid difficulty.
- End each day by recalling a moment of defiant hope, a time you kept going even when you wanted to quit.

Embracing both the gifts God has entrusted to you and the journey of resilience, you establish a foundation for excellence. Next, the focus will uncover the subtle enemies of progress, laziness and procrastination, and equip you to guard your impact through disciplined habits and purposeful priorities.

 Breaking Patterns: Excellence vs. Laziness and Procrastination

The Spirit of God activates gifts in every believer with purpose attached. Those gifts are never meant for idle admiration or selfish gain. They are meant for action, active service, bold obedience, and real transformation in the lives of others. Yet even the most anointed gifts become dull where passivity, laziness, or procrastination are allowed to linger. The cost of wasted potential is not just personal disappointment; it affects the advance of the kingdom itself.

Consider what happens when passivity takes root. The wise teacher in Proverbs 24:30–34 describes walking by the field of the sluggard: thorns had grown everywhere, the ground lay unkempt, the stone wall broken down. For a time, seeds of talent or faith might remain hidden beneath the surface, but neglect will always reveal itself eventually. It often starts quietly, skipping a meeting, overlooking a deadline, neglecting prayer or preparation "just this once." As those moments stack up, skills dwindle, trust erodes, and previously open doors close. Unused gifts atrophy like unused muscles, leaving behind spiritual erosion much harder to repair.

Laziness is more than a bad habit. It's a theft from the future God calls us to build. Every assignment, relationship, and opportunity handed to you is a trust to be stewarded. When you neglect these, you do not merely let yourself down; you rob the church, your workplace, your family, and the generation after you. Mediocrity is a slow fade, not a sudden collapse. Over time, families grow distant, ministries lose momentum, and once-promising careers flatten. No amount of natural gifting can make up for a lack of applied effort and focus.

Procrastination masquerades as mere forgetfulness or busyness, but God's Word reveals its deeper danger. James 4:17 states, *"If anyone knows the good they ought to do, and doesn't do it, it is sin for them."* Postponement is a spiritual battle cloaked in excuses. A Christian leader who delays addressing a team issue may avoid conflict briefly but soon faces greater breakdown and distrust. A business professional who keeps putting off a proposal or stewardship of finances finds opportunities slipping away or potential lost. Deferring God's promptings is not a scheduling issue; it reveals a heart issue, one in which fear, comfort, and self-doubt override conviction.

Conviction, not convenience, must drive the decisions of a believer. Following feelings and the urgencies imposed by others leads to constant drifting. Emotionally driven choices leave you vulnerable to every wind and tide. People will always have expectations: invitations to serve on committees, requests to volunteer, opportunities that may even seem good. Even Jesus modelled strategic focus.

Mind His Business Not Theirs

He went to only one wedding recorded in His ministry, the wedding at Cana, choosing assignments with clarity and purpose rather than scattering Himself thin.

When you allow conviction to define your calendar and commitments, the urgent distractions begin to lose their grip. The youth pastor called mainly to discipleship resists the pressure to take on another program simply for visibility. The Christian entrepreneur learns to say "no" to every potential partnership, focusing energy where fruit can truly grow. In the marketplace, the follower of Jesus sets boundaries so that essential work and relationships take priority over busywork or well-intentioned distractions. Excellence is rarely about the spotlight. The most transformative acts of faithfulness often happen with no applause, no stage, and sometimes no immediate results. Many Christians grow weary because they hunger for recognition, but this craving leads to exhaustion and disappointment when praise does not come. The kingdom prize belongs to those who steward well in secret, the assistant who prepares the pastor's materials without public acknowledgment, the parent who prays fervently at bedtime, the employee who quietly honours God with diligence even when the boss is away. Scripture elevates these acts, reminding us that God notices what people miss.

The call is to search your motives honestly. Are you cutting corners when no one is looking? Are you waiting for the "perfect moment" to do what you know is right? The path away from mediocrity and into excellence begins with disciplined routines. Simple daily habits, setting a time for undistracted devotion, planning your work ahead, choosing to address responsibilities first, build momentum and clarity. Wise stewardship is not accidental; it is forged through intention, planning, and prioritisation.

A spirit of discipline safeguards your calling and magnifies your impact. Smart routines, chosen systems, and tools that support focus help you honour each role God gives. As you build these habits, you free your gifts to flourish and position yourself for greater productivity and lasting, spiritual fruitfulness. The next step involves unpacking specific strategies and healthy rhythms of work and rest that empower you to live and lead with true excellence, both in God's sight and for the world He sends you to serve.

Productivity Tips & Modern Hacks for Excellence

To pursue godly excellence is to work wholeheartedly, not settling for "good enough" when God calls for faithfulness and diligence. Scripture urges:

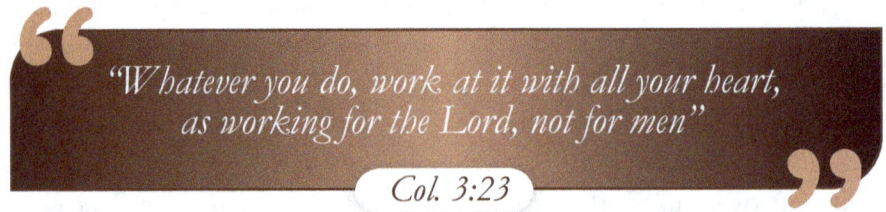

> "Whatever you do, work at it with all your heart, as working for the Lord, not for men"
> *Col. 3:23*

Excellence begins with this conviction, energised by grace and practical, wise systems, not just willpower. The right tools and rhythms serve as channels for God's purposes, ensuring that faith-inspired intentions become measurable outcomes in both church and marketplace.

 ## Time Blocking for Focused Stewardship

Time blocking is a biblical response to scattered attention, echoing the wisdom to "number our days that we may gain a heart of wisdom" (Ps. 90:12). This method equips believers to dedicate specific hours to their assignments, avoiding drift and distraction.

- Review upcoming priorities for the week each Sunday.
- Assign specific time slots in your calendar to each project, meeting, or responsibility.
- Dedicate "deep work" blocks where you mute devices and close nonessential tabs.
- Leave space for rest and prayer, treating these appointments as non-negotiable.

Picture a ministry director responsible for sermon prep, counselling, and event planning. She blocks out Monday mornings for undistracted study, afternoons for meetings, and Fridays for outreach visits. Interruptions dwindle, projects stop feeling overwhelming, and the quality of both preaching and care improves as her focus honours God's call.

The 2-Minute Rule: Honouring Small Tasks

Proverbs teaches that steady diligence yields reward (Prov. 13:4). The 2-minute rule ensures Christians don't waste energy postponing what could be accomplished immediately, freeing mental space for weightier assignments.

- Whenever a new task or email appears, ask if it takes less than 2 minutes.
- If so, complete it right then, don't delay or overthink.
- If it requires more time, add it to a prioritised list for scheduled work blocks.

A Christian consultant receives several quick client requests in the morning. Instead of letting them stack up, he handles password resets, call scheduling, and brief emails as each arises. This stewardship reduces clutter, strengthens his testimony, and creates margin for creative, strategic work.

Prioritisation Techniques for God-Honouring Impact

Turning intentions into impact requires more than lists; it calls for wise choice. Jesus Himself was purposeful, focusing on the most essential mission moments. Employ proven tools like the Eisenhower Matrix or Ivy Lee Method:

- Write down every task or project for your week.
- Label each as urgent/important, not urgent/important, urgent/not important, or neither.
- Schedule highest-priority ("urgent and important") tasks for your best energy periods.
- Delegate or eliminate lower-priority activities.

Mind His Business Not Theirs

A Christian business leader faces a product launch, staffing concerns, and donor reports. She uses the Eisenhower Matrix to clarify that launch planning and donor updates come first each day, while less critical tasks wait until later. This brings calm, enables better results, and models gospel-centred stewardship.

 ### Digital Tools for Multiplied Capacity

Wise use of technology is a modern expression of stewardship. Apps like Notion and Trello let believers organise projects, track goals, and share updates with teams. AI tools, including ChatGPT for research or Grammarly for communications, polish output and save time

- Choose one main app for planning (e.g., Notion/Trello) and set up boards for each responsibility.
- Use categories like "urgent," "in progress," and "waiting" to move projects visually.
- For recurring communications, apply Grammarly or a template to produce excellent, clear writing.
- Try an AI-powered planner or research tool to prepare for meetings or sermons in minutes.

A youth pastor tracks his multi-camp schedule, lesson outlines, and parent communications on Notion. He delegates assignments with Trello, while Grammarly ensures newsletters are clear and error-free. His congregation perceives not just organisation, but loving, intentional leadership.

 ### Digital Boundaries and Decluttered Attention

Modern distractions threaten single-minded devotion. Proverbs 4:23 reminds us to guard the heart. Intentional boundaries restore focus and help believers remain present to God and people.

- Set phone to "Do Not Disturb" mode during deep work or prayer periods.

- Silence or mute nonessential notification channels (social media, group chats).
- Schedule a weekly tech "fast", one evening or a full Sabbath, away from screens.
- Unsubscribe from distracting email lists or unnecessary subscriptions.

A Christian nonprofit director introduces "focus hours" free from digital interruptions. Team members report stronger collaboration and energy, rediscovering space for reflection and spiritual growth alongside their tasks.

 ### Rest-Rhythms: Excellence Flows from Sabbath

True excellence blends doing and resting, following God's pattern:

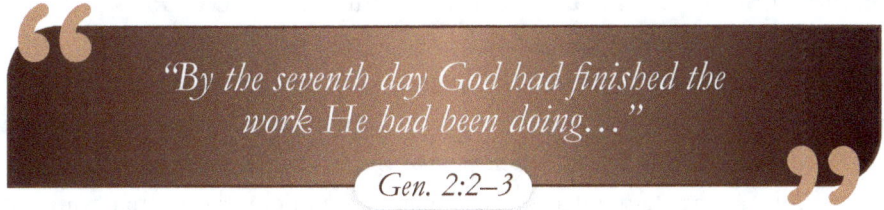

> *"By the seventh day God had finished the work He had been doing…"*
> Gen. 2:2–3

Sabbath is not an afterthought but a fuel for productivity and spiritual vitality.

- Schedule a 24-hour Sabbath on your calendar.
- Prepare tasks in advance so work will not intrude.
- Inform colleagues and loved ones about this commitment.
- Choose practices on Sabbath that restore (worship, art, nature, time with family).

A Christian CEO leaves email behind every Sunday, spends time in worship, and enjoys a long walk with family. The renewal she experiences pours back into her leadership, fostering clarity, patience, and fresh vision for her calling. Productivity is just the beginning; as the work takes shape, so does your legacy, bearing fruit that others will inherit for God's glory.

Legacy Building: Creating Lasting Impact

Building a legacy goes beyond personal accomplishment or fleeting recognition. In the biblical sense, legacy means investing in work or lives that point to God and remain fruitful long after one's direct involvement ends. This kind of inheritance mirrors Jesus' words in John 15:16, describing the call to bear "fruit that will last." Such lasting fruit takes many practical shapes: changed lives, enduring kingdom systems, and the multiplication of new leaders.

 ## Practical Fruit: Changed Lives and Systems

The impact of a life committed to God is ultimately measured by transformation in others and systems that continue to serve God's purposes. A business that operates with integrity and generosity, a ministry that lifts up the marginalised, or a mentoring relationship that produces new leaders are all forms of fruit. Real legacy is less about what is accumulated and more about who and what is being developed to outlast personal presence.

For example, a Christian entrepreneur may build an enterprise that continues to provide fair employment and opportunities for years, even as leadership transitions. Consistent excellence in small daily tasks contributes to this, as every relationship and project can lay a brick in the foundation for future generations.

 ## Multiplication Through Mentoring

Scripture puts multiplication at the heart of mission. In 2 Timothy 2:2, Paul exhorts Timothy, *"What you have heard from me in the presence of many witnesses entrust to faithful people who will be able to teach others also."* This creates a four-generation chain: Paul to Timothy, Timothy to trusted others, and these to future teachers.

Mentoring is intentional and relational. It involves seeing beyond the moment and investing time to build both skills and character in others. In any context: church, business, home, or marketplace, multiplying means identifying those who are teachable, committed, and demonstrate the capacity to grow and lead.

Start by asking who around you is hungry to learn and serve, attentive to correction, and consistent in small things. Notice who takes initiative, receives feedback well, and desires to honour God in their work. It is not always the most outspoken or gifted, but often those who combine humility with reliability.

 ### How to Equip and Multiply

Growing others requires structure. Regular check-ins, shared projects, and space for honest questions build trust. Share both successes and failures so mentees learn how to navigate challenges.

Set clear goals for learning, perhaps teaching a skill, passing on an organisational process, or exploring a foundational spiritual discipline. Provide practical resources and progressively give increasing responsibility.

In the marketplace, kingdom multiplication might look like training a core team to serve with excellence, then releasing them to lead new efforts. In the church, it might mean discipling new believers and equipping them to teach and mentor others. At home, it could mean modelling and discussing faith, discipline, and service with children or family.

 ### Living for Eternal Results

Decisions shaped by eternal perspective look different from those driven by short-term gains. When eternity is the goal, daily work carries deeper significance. Choosing honesty over shortcuts, honouring commitments, and serving quietly without recognition reflect a heart set on outcomes that may not be visible now but carry weight in God's kingdom.

Imagine a manager who spends extra time developing a struggling team member. Although this may not earn immediate praise or increase short-term profit, the effort's value emerges over time as the individual grows and eventually mentors others. The ripple effect reaches far, especially when motivated by a desire to honour God rather than impress others.

Scripture frames this pursuit: Colossians 3:23 urges, *""Whatever you do, work at it with all your heart, as working for the Lord, not for human masters."* In practical terms, this means evaluating each task, decision, or conflict with a question, how will this impact eternity?

 Recording the Journey

A legacy gains real power when documented and shared. Recording testimonies, milestones, and lessons learned makes the pathway visible and practical for others. This can take several forms:

- **Journaling:** Noting breakthroughs, significant conversations, and answered prayers provides a personal record of God's faithfulness.
- **Digital archives:** Compiling project notes, team reflections, or key outcomes in shared documents ensures that knowledge endures.
- **Storytelling sessions:** Gathering a group to share experiences and testimonies cements wisdom and reinforces shared values.

These records serve as blueprints for others to follow, adapt, and build upon. They also remind leaders and teams of God's guidance and provision in challenging seasons. Making this documentation a regular rhythm helps each new generation pick up the mission with confidence and clarity.

 **Final Thoughts**

Now that we understand how spiritual partnership, disciplined effort, and practical tools combine to fuel excellence, we can move forward with renewed purpose and clarity. Embracing the Holy Spirit's empowerment transforms every task into worship and opens the door for gifts to flourish even amid challenges. When we acknowledge His presence in our work, even the smallest assignment takes on eternal weight and significance. No longer do we simply complete tasks to meet deadlines or impress others; instead, every action becomes an offering of obedience that carries the fragrance of devotion to God.

At the same time, excellence requires more than inspiration. It calls for deliberate, disciplined effort. By rejecting passivity and procrastination, and by stewarding our talents with intentional focus, we position ourselves to make a lasting impact that extends far beyond immediate results. This kind of diligence reflects the nature of Christ Himself, who declared that He must be about His Father's business. The pursuit of excellence in any sphere of life, whether in business, ministry, creativity, or family, is not simply about achievement, it is about alignment with heaven's mandate.

This chapter equips you not only to finish what God has set before you but also to build a legacy of faithfulness, resilience, and multiplication. Faithfulness ensures that you do not abandon your assignment when it becomes difficult. Resilience keeps you pressing forward when resistance arises. Multiplication guarantees that what God has entrusted to you produces fruit that benefits others and extends His kingdom. To live this way is to participate in a rhythm of grace and responsibility, where your obedience to God creates ripples that influence generations.

Mind His Business Not Theirs

As you apply these principles, your daily work, whether in church, in business, or in the home, will increasingly reflect God's kingdom values and bear fruit that endures into eternity. When you embrace this mindset, you begin to see challenges not as roadblocks but as opportunities for growth. You no longer measure your progress solely by visible results but by the faithfulness of your stewardship. This is the path to true excellence: a life where the Spirit's empowerment, your disciplined effort, and practical wisdom converge to create impact that glorifies God and transforms lives.

SECTION 3

EMBRACING THE PURPOSE OF GOD

Mind His Business Not Theirs

Now that you have broken free from self-sabotage and learned to rise above the opinions of men, you are standing at a pivotal place in your journey. You are free. Free from the internal chains that held you back. Free from the pressures of approval. Free from the weight of other people's expectations. But freedom is not the final destination. Freedom is preparation. It is the launchpad for something far greater. It is the opportunity to step fully into the purpose that God has designed specifically for your life. This is the moment when the journey of self-discovery transforms into a journey of destiny.

The purpose of God is not something incidental or accidental. It was determined from the foundations of the earth. Before you existed, before the world itself was fully formed, God had a mission for you. The Bible tells us in Ephesians 2:10 that *"we are God's workmanship, created in Christ Jesus for good works, which God prepared in advance for us to do."* Every person has tasks, assignments, and missions that are unique to them. These assignments are designed to reveal the reign and power of Jesus Christ on the earth in ways that no one else can. They are specifically for you. Your life contains treasures hidden by design, waiting for you to discover. Scripture tells us that we have this treasure hidden in earthen vessels. God's purpose is often concealed, not to frustrate you, but to protect it from the enemy. It is kept safe until you are ready to steward it faithfully.

Discovering your purpose is not about immediate gratification or worldly gain. It is about uncovering the beauty, the gifts, the talents, and the spiritual assignments that God has planted within you. Your purpose is a treasure to be discovered. It is hidden, not on the surface of your life, but deep within you. That is why the Bible compares it to treasure hidden in earthen vessels. God hides these treasures so that the enemy cannot steal, distort, or diminish the impact of your life. You have to actively seek, explore, and discover what is within you. It is a journey of revelation.

Discovering your purpose is not about immediate gratification or worldly gain. It is uncovering the beauty, the gifts, the talents, and the spiritual assignments that God has planted within you. Your purpose is a treasure to be discovered. It is hidden, not on the surface of your life, but deep within you. That is why the Bible compares it to treasure hidden in earthen vessels. God hides these treasures so that the enemy cannot steal, distort, or diminish the impact of your life. You have to actively seek, explore, and discover what is within you. It is a journey of revelation.

Your journey of purpose operates step by step. As with Abraham, God does not reveal everything at once. When God called Abraham, He said, *"Come up from your land and I will show you the land."* The first step was obedience. Abraham could not see the entirety of God's plan, but he had to trust and act on what God revealed in the present. Only after taking the first step would God reveal the next.

The same principle applies to your life. If you resist the first step, you will remain in the same place, wondering what God has for you. Purpose unfolds progressively. Step one leads to step two. Step two leads to step three, and before you know it, you are walking fully in the mission for which you were created.

You are like a bird that has been trained to fly. You have learned the discipline, the strength, and the patience required to soar. Now it is time to lift off, to spread your wings, and to embrace the mission for which you were created. Purpose is not passive. It requires partnership, action, and trust. It requires that you lean into the Holy Spirit, who is given to guide, strengthen, and empower you as you execute the assignments God has placed in your life. Romans 8:11 tells us that *"the same Spirit who raised Jesus from the dead dwells in us and will give life to our mortal bodies."* The Spirit enables, quickens, and strengthens us to fulfil God's work with endurance, wisdom, and power. Purpose becomes attainable when we cooperate with the Spirit's guidance and trust His direction.

Purpose is anchored in the eternal. It is bigger than any temporary blessing or earthly achievement. Material success, possessions, relationships, and recognition are all gifts, but they are not the ultimate reward.

The true reward is eternal. It is the reward of having laboured faithfully in the kingdom of God, fulfilling your calling, and hearing the words, *"Well done, good and faithful servant."* Scripture reminds us in 1 Corinthians 3:13-14 that each person's work will be tested by fire, and the quality of that work will determine the reward we receive. Paul, in 2 Timothy 2:4, also reminds us that *"a soldier does not entangle himself with civilian affairs but strives to please the one who enlisted him."* Similarly, our lives are meant to focus on the eternal. We must not be distracted by temporary comforts or fleeting accolades. We are here to serve, to fulfil God's plan, and to prioritise heaven above the earth. When heaven is the focus, all earthly blessings become byproducts of faithful obedience and alignment with God's purpose.

Your purpose is discovered and nurtured through intentionality. It requires living a life set apart, consecrated for God's work, and willing to be used wherever He calls you. The Holy Spirit equips you with discernment, wisdom, and strength to navigate challenges, to build and execute plans, and to walk confidently into every assignment. God does not leave us to accomplish His purposes in our own strength. Philippians 2:13 tells us that *"it is God who works in us both to will and to act according to His good pleasure."* The Spirit empowers us to accomplish what the Father has prepared, giving capacity and insight beyond what our human understanding can produce.

Understanding and embracing God's purpose also requires trust in His timing. Life unfolds in seasons. Each season equips you for the next. What you do today lays the foundation for tomorrow's revelation. As you continue to break free from self-sabotage and rise above the opinions of men, you are learning obedience and faith. Each act of faith, no matter how small, unlocks the next assignment. Gifts hidden within you begin to surface. Opportunities open in confirmation of God's hand at work in your life. As you progress, the treasures within you become evident, and your life begins to reflect the Kingdom of God in ways that are tangible, impactful, and enduring.

Biblical examples reinforce this principle. Joseph, betrayed by his brothers, sold into slavery, and imprisoned for a crime he did not commit, remained steadfast in his faith. His obedience and trust in God's purpose ultimately led to the salvation of nations. Moses, despite fear and hesitation, embraced God's calling to lead Israel out of Egypt. Paul, once a persecutor of Christians, became a powerful vessel for the Gospel, leaving a legacy that shaped the world. Each of these men faced uncertainty, fear, and opposition. Each could have been distracted by circumstances, opinions, or self-doubt. Yet their lives demonstrate that when we align ourselves with God's purpose, trust His timing, and walk in obedience, the mission unfolds with power, clarity, and fruitfulness.

Even modern research supports this reality. Studies in positive psychology and neuroscience show that people who pursue a clear sense of purpose experience higher levels of resilience, mental clarity, and well-being. Purpose shapes decision-making, builds motivation, and strengthens perseverance. When we anchor our identity in God's eternal design, our confidence is no longer dependent on circumstances or the opinions of others. Our minds are renewed, and our actions reflect consistency, focus, and alignment with divine destiny. Purpose, therefore, is both spiritual and practical. It impacts every area of life, mentally, emotionally, spiritually, and physically.

Finally, embracing God's purpose is about keeping the eternal perspective in focus. It is about working for a reward that cannot fade, a legacy that endures beyond the temporary concerns of this life. Finishing well is not about the recognition, comfort, or even influence you may gain on earth. It is about pleasing God and faithfully stewarding the mission He has entrusted to you. Heaven before earth. Eternal reward before temporary gain. By keeping this perspective, every choice, effort, and sacrifice becomes meaningful. Every assignment, whether in ministry, business, family, or community, becomes part of a greater story, your story, written in alignment with God's eternal plan.

Mind His Business Not Theirs

You are not here merely to exist. You are here to discover, to steward, and to operate in the fullness of God's plan for your life. As you step into this season, remember that purpose is a journey, not a single revelation. Each day offers the opportunity to uncover more of the treasures hidden within you, to walk in partnership with the Holy Spirit, and to focus on the eternal reward that awaits those who remain faithful. You have been trained to fly. You have been prepared, refined, and equipped. Now it is time to soar. Now it is time to step fully into the divine assignment that has been uniquely prepared for you, confident that God will lead
you every step of the way.

KEY 7

WALKING IN THE FATHER'S LOVE

*Drink deeply of the Father's love,
and watch it overflow, healing,
bridging and giving courage where
fear once ruled*

Philip Dada Jr

Mind His Business Not Theirs

"She just doesn't seem to care," Mark muttered under his breath after yet another tense meeting with a colleague who constantly challenged and criticised his ideas. He wanted to respond firmly, even sharply, but found himself holding back, uncertain how to maintain peace without giving in or becoming resentful. At home, Mary felt the weight of unspoken distance growing between her and a family member who had withdrawn after a hurtful disagreement. She longed to bridge the gap but wasn't sure where to begin or if her efforts would be met with openness. These moments, when love feels complicated by frustration, misunderstanding, or exhaustion, are familiar to many who seek to live out their faith in real life. The struggle isn't simply feeling loved; it's learning how to let that love shape responses, rebuild relationships, and inspire courage every day amid challenges that test patience and grace.

Becoming a Conduit, Not Just a Container

Learning to walk in the Father's love begins with intentionally receiving it, not as a one-time event but as an ongoing posture of the heart. Daily moments of meditation, worship, prayer, or silent reflection open space within us to sense God's approval and nearness, making His love more than a distant doctrine. These rhythms are as essential to spiritual vitality as breathing is to life. Without attending to God's affection, our efforts to pass on love to others soon feel mechanical or far too costly, because we are drawing from an empty reservoir. Love that is first received becomes a living wellspring, flowing authentically to those around us, not out of obligation or a need to earn favour, but as a heartfelt response to what we have already been given.

Consider the business leader who starts mornings in stillness, reading and repeating scriptural affirmations such as "I have loved you with an everlasting love" or "Nothing can separate us from the love of God." Throughout the day, setbacks or unexpected challenges may arise, harsh criticism on a project, short tempers in a meeting, pressures to compromise for quick results. Instead of reacting defensively or allowing stress to dictate actions, the leader remembers those morning truths.

Remaining conscious of being loved by God, grace and patience are extended, even under pressure. This shift fuels decisions and interactions, affecting not only workload but workplace relationships and morale.

While steady receiving is foundational, the Father's love transforms most deeply as it is extended in real time especially toward those who test us. Every Christian knows the challenge of loving difficult individuals: the colleague who constantly interrupts, the church member who is slow to forgive, the neighbour who seems impossible to please. Extending grace in these moments mirrors the very heart of God. One practical blueprint: begin with prayer for the person, setting aside personal frustrations to ask God for His view on their situation. Explore what unseen struggles or stresses might be shaping their behaviour, not to excuse wrong but to respond with clarity instead of raw emotion. Select a single meaningful action, offering a genuine word of encouragement when criticism might be expected or taking time to listen fully before asserting a point in a tense discussion.

Imagine a workplace scenario where a team member subtly undermines your contributions, perhaps out of insecurity or resentment. The natural reaction is to guard yourself or return the negativity. Choosing instead to speak a kind word about their strengths, or assist during a tight deadline, disrupts the cycle and plants seeds of trust. Through consistent, intentional acts of empathy, the pattern of Christ's love takes root in difficult soil, shifting the emotional climate over time.

The journey from internalising love to making it tangible is marked by small, consistent actions. It does not depend on charismatic gestures but on regular, attentive care. At home, work, or church, remembering a colleague's family need or pausing to listen to a friend's burden, signals value and communicates the Father's heart. Simple habits such as crafting a thank-you note, helping with a mundane task, or showing up on time, have a compounding effect. When frustration or impatience would normally control a conversation, instead extending gentle attention signals which voice we serve. In families, pausing the rush to listen to a child's story, or quietly supporting a spouse's efforts, makes invisible love visible.

Mind His Business Not Theirs

Sustaining this lifestyle requires vigilance against the drain of burnout. A pattern of giving, divorced from God's presence will eventually leave us depleted, serving out of exhaustion rather than joy. Prayer, reflection, and worship are not extra demands, but vital replenishment. Embracing rhythms of rest such as digital detox days, personal retreats, or simply setting aside regular hours for silence, protects capacity and preserves joy in service. Picture the pastor or entrepreneur who guards time each week to switch off devices, retreat, and soak in scripture; when regular responsibilities resume, their well is full, and love flows out rather than leaks. Participation in faith-centred small groups or accountability partnerships fortifies this lifestyle, offering encouragement and refreshment.

To plant these truths, a simple self-help exercise can bridge belief to practical action:

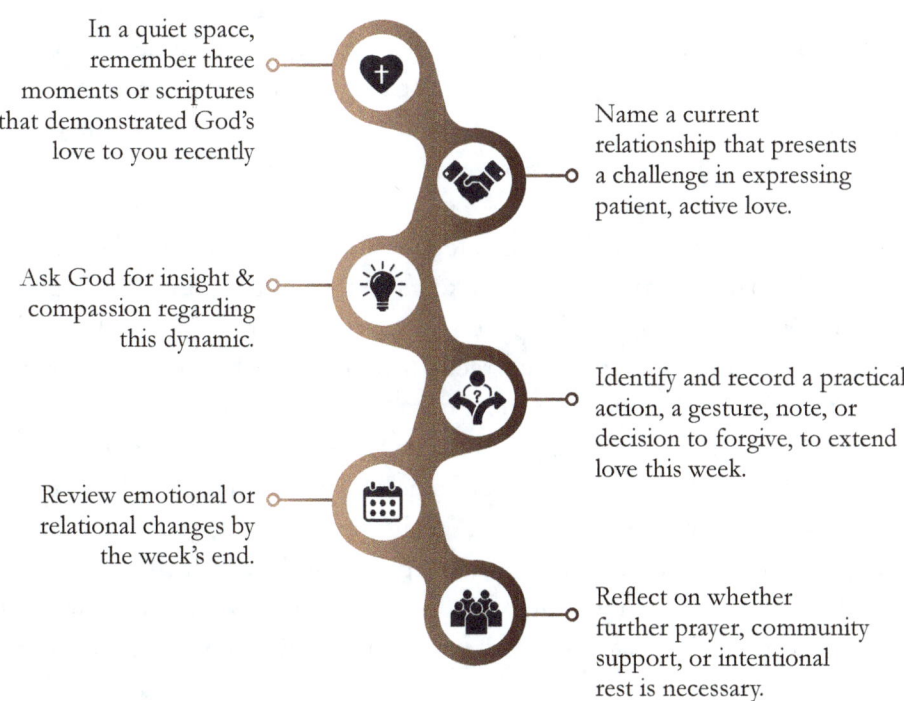

- In a quiet space, remember three moments or scriptures that demonstrated God's love to you recently
- Name a current relationship that presents a challenge in expressing patient, active love.
- Ask God for insight & compassion regarding this dynamic.
- Identify and record a practical action, a gesture, note, or decision to forgive, to extend love this week.
- Review emotional or relational changes by the week's end.
- Reflect on whether further prayer, community support, or intentional rest is necessary.

This steady journey, from receiving to authentically
giving, lays the groundwork for more radical, everyday expressions of the kingdom's love that will soon be explored in greater depth.

 ## Radical Kindness as a Kingdom Strategy

Every person we meet, whether in a boardroom, checkout line, living room, or church foyer, offers an invitation to embody God's love. When daily encounters become holy opportunities, even work emails, neighbourhood hellos, and family dinners feel different. This mindset realigns simple moments as ministry, urging us toward active kingdom participation instead of settling for passive observance.

Kindness loses none of its strength by being small or ordinary. Jesus himself noticed overlooked people, wiped away shame with gentle words, and dignified the unremarkable with his touch. When a leader thanks a janitor by name, or a parent pauses to listen instead of hurrying away, heaven's culture enters hidden spaces. Whispered apologies, a patient tone in the face of irritation, or remembering a coworker's struggle with a text or coffee, these ministry moments flow quietly yet steadily. Their value is not measured by applause or attention but by the love that motivates them.

A nurse paused in a busy hallway, offering her sandwich to a tired security guard who hadn't eaten. Neither spoke more than a few words, but the guard later confided that hope had slipped back into his evening. In another office, a manager resisted the urge to correct a team member harshly after a failed presentation and instead wrote her a note praising her initiative, offering feedback later in private. The humiliation that usually followed public mistakes lessened. Sarcasm and silent tension faded. One act of kindness softened the workplace atmosphere, emails grew warmer, people lingered longer to help one another. At home, a spouse washed their partner's car after a hard week, leaving a handwritten scripture in the console. Tears welled up, not because the task was grand, but because it was timed with real need.

Simple kindness wields power as spiritual warfare. Bitterness and hostility thrive on neglect, but loving gestures disrupt these cycles, no matter how subtle. When a churchgoer repeatedly greeted an irritable neighbour, week after week, the walls fell. Over time, the neighbour began sharing struggles that no sermon could have reached. The act was unseen by most, but the ripple effect, a family invited to church, a broken friendship mended, was unmistakable.

Unexpected blessings frequently spring from such moments. After paying for a stranger's groceries, a believer received a note weeks later: "Your kindness restored my faith when I'd almost given up. I started praying again." Another time, a barista's sincere compliment about someone's patience in a long line prompted a conversation about faith outside the café on a chilly morning. The relationship grew. These stories suggest that God multiplies what we offer. The moments are not wasted, even when effect is hidden.

 Daily Kindness Challenge: 30 Days of Intentional Love

Adults longing to move from theory to practice can harness a tangible daily habit by committing to the following detailed steps for 30 days.

1. **Begin Each Morning in Prayer**
   Before the day starts, ask God to reveal moments, people, and spaces where kindness could make kingdom impact. Request a heart alert to urgent needs and   subtle opportunities.

2. **Choose a Daily Act of Kindness**
   Identify one intentional, practical gesture to extend, suited to your context:

   - Write a note of appreciation to a teacher, coworker, or mentor.
   - Leave an encouraging card on a neighbour's doorstep.
   - Buy coffee for the person behind you in line.
   - Offer extra support to an overwhelmed colleague by taking on a task.
   - Invite a quiet group member to join your lunch table.
   - Lend a listening ear to a family member without rushing or judgment.

- Offer to pray with a friend or colleague who seems discouraged.
- Share honest thanks with service staff at a grocery store.
- Text someone who is isolated, reminding them they're not forgotten.

3. **Kindness Journal Entry**

    At day's end, write a short account: the act chosen, what stirred your heart, any response or change noticed, internal or external.

Example Entry 1:

Act: Sent a message of encouragement to my boss after a tough meeting. Motivation: Felt prompted during my morning prayer. Response: He replied with gratitude, surprised I noticed his mood. It made me more aware of how leadership also needs support.

Example Entry 2:

Act: Held the door for a frazzled mom at church and offered to watch her toddler while she found her seat. Motivation: Awareness of her exhaustion. Response: She looked relieved and thanked me quietly. It softened my own impatience before the service.

4. **Evening Reflection**

    Finish with honest reflection:
    - How did choosing kindness affect your emotions, stress, or interactions?
    - Was it natural, or did you need to push past reluctance?
    - Did your awareness of God's presence with you change?

Practical kindness grows easier and less self-conscious with repetition. Over time, the habit forms a default setting, leaving less room for complacency. Some days bring immediate fruit, a restored friendship, relief in a tense room. Other times, the results remain hidden, requiring continued faith that God is at work multiplying each seed sown.

Soon, your journey will move deeper, exploring how the supernatural and emotional power of God's love restores and reconciles beyond simple acts.

Healing Through Love

Acts of kindness serve as the foundation for healing, often silent but undeniable in their influence. When a gentle word or thoughtful gesture is offered repeatedly, these actions begin to work on the stony soil of hurt and mistrust. For example, someone may keep showing up for a friend who has withdrawn after disappointment, bringing a cup of coffee or writing a simple note that says, "I care." In time, these small seeds of kindness sprout, creating visible cracks in walls that once seemed impenetrable. Over several months, the friend gradually opens up, giving voice to pain, and the relationship is built back, one gentle act at a time. Consistent expressions of care convey a message: "You are valuable, even if you cannot give anything in return right now." Small, thoughtful actions wear down bitterness and suspicion, signalling safety and restoring hope to relationships once marked by sorrow or distance.

Compassion goes beyond kindness by meeting people in the depth of their need. A compassionate presence does not shrink from another's grief, shame, or fear. In families where a child has withdrawn after a season of rebellion, a parent who sits and listens, without jumping to conclusions or doling out judgment, offers a safe space for vulnerability. The child, sensing there is no threat of condemnation, may begin to speak honestly. This kind of attentive love gently dissolves anxiety and scepticism. Compassion is the force that reaches across emotional chasms, bridging divides with patience and humility. In a workplace wracked by competition and misunderstanding, one manager saw her team unravel after a project failure. Determined to shift the atmosphere, she consistently asked her team members about their lives and thanked them for their efforts. Over weeks, suspicion faded, and team morale grew. Her willingness to acknowledge pain and honour effort rebuilt connections. Compassion brings hidden wounds into the light, creating opportunities for healing to take root in even the most fractured settings.

Forgiveness stands as the cornerstone of restoration, breaking cycles of resentment that smother growth. Unlike forgetting or excusing wrongs, forgiveness requires choosing to release the debt others owe due to their mistakes. It is an act of surrender, often undertaken before one's emotions catch up. When a long-standing friend betrayed her years ago, one woman wrestled for months with anger and heartache. Yet she chose to forgive daily, praying for her friend and wishing her well, even through tears. This intentional release melted the bitterness that had begun to harden her heart. Eventually, they spoke honestly about the pain. The act of forgiving paved a path for reconciliation as they rebuilt trust through honest dialogue and renewed boundaries. Forgiveness uproots the thorns of offence, offering fresh soil for genuine peace and renewed intimacy. In every act of mercy, believers mirror the Father's heart, revealing a supernatural love that overcomes human frailty.

Loving communication wields the power to restore and give life. Words can either deepen wounds or patch them together with hope. In families where harsh criticism has created distance, sincere affirmation breaks the pattern. Consider a father who, after years of sharp words, began each morning telling his daughter something he admired in her character. Where shame once lingered, the daughter found courage and self-worth rising within. Loving speech means choosing to speak the truth but always doing so for the purpose of building up. A manager who openly praised an employee's integrity in front of colleagues saw that person's confidence return and performance improve. Affirmation cancels out negative voices from the past and affirms a person's true value and purpose. Reconciliation often begins with words mending hearts and repairing relationships that have endured years of misunderstanding.

Testimonies abound of relationships renewed through persistent love. In small groups, stories are shared of couples who once felt hopeless growing close again after practicing daily forgiveness and encouragement. An employee recounts how a supervisor's consistent encouragement and refusal to gossip restored her confidence and trust in leadership.

A community leader testifies of a decades-old feud ending with a handwritten letter of apology and an invitation to dinner, turning former adversaries into allies for neighbourhood outreach. Each testimony reveals the transformative effect of love put into action, softening hearts, healing painful histories, and drawing people together in unity.

Sometimes, love calls for wisdom in order to remain strong. After years of rebuilding a broken friendship, one woman realised that continuing reconciliation would mean setting healthier boundaries, both for her own well-being and for the good of the relationship. She reached out with kindness but also chose honesty, learning to say no when needed. This allowed trust to flourish without resentment. Wise love, patient and discerning, sustains both restoration and health for the long term.

 Boundaries Without Bitterness

Expressions of compassion, trust, and restoration shape relationships and repair what has been broken. These qualities, while transformative, do not thrive in the absence of personal boundaries. For love to do its healing work, it must sometimes take the form of a respectful "no," a line drawn with gentleness and courage. Relationships built solely on forgiveness or compassion, but lacking boundaries, risk falling into familiar cycles of disappointment, resentment, and even harm. Boundaries, then, serve not as barriers to love, but as guardians of dignity and hope.

A common misconception holds that Christian love erases all limits, suggesting that endurance is endless, patience knows no end, and generosity disregards personal cost. This idea quietly encourages self-neglect or even enables unhealthy patterns in the name of faithfulness. In truth, love flourishes when it operates within safe, honest boundaries. Consider the believer who repeatedly forgives a dismissive coworker. Forgiveness can become a bridge for restored trust; but if the disrespect continues unchecked, the workplace grows tense and the believer grows exhausted, eventually feeling incapable of reflecting Christ's presence at all.

Healthy boundaries shift this pattern. By confidently and kindly addressing the behaviour, the believer offers both justice and mercy, not only preserving their own wellbeing but also creating space for the coworker to grow.

Boundaries are not rejections of others; they are invitations to mutual respect. Whenever someone encounters behaviour that drains joy or undermines peace, the loving response may require stating their need rather than simply absorbing the impact. Relational wholeness depends on this balance of openhearted grace and honest self-respect. Imagine a friend who often turns your conversations into complaints or venting sessions. Each time, you listen out of care but notice your own spirit dragging afterward. To continue in this unending role might seem loving, but it quietly chips away at your emotional reserve and closes the door to healthy encouragement. Instead, acknowledging the pattern and expressing a need for change allows both friends to find renewal. A gentle, clear statement "I care about you deeply, but I'm not able to take on this much right now. Can we focus on supporting each other in new ways?" models love that is both open and wise.

 ## Communicating Boundaries with Grace

Asserting boundaries does not require bluntness or a rigid tone. Christ-centred communication flows from a heart that values both truth and relationship. When someone needs to express a limit, words matter not only in meaning, but in manner. A believer might say, "I value our friendship, but I can't keep saying yes to late-night calls when I have early workdays," or "I respect your leadership, but I need to clarify what I am able to take on in this season." Such statements remain firm without hostility, anchoring the conversation in goodwill and mutual respect.

For those in leadership or workplace roles, the call to compassion may feel at odds with the necessity to correct or redirect. Yet strong leaders recognise the spiritual importance of healthy boundaries. A Christian supervisor, for example, may need to address repeated tardiness with an employee.

Compassion invites understanding, but accountability demands clarity: "I appreciate your dedication to our team and want you to thrive here. Regular attendance is needed for our work together. How can we support you in this area?" These words aim not for reprimand, but for collaboration and honest growth.

Sometimes love prescribes distance rather than ongoing interaction. There are seasons when the most caring step is to step away, to allow healing or change to happen apart from daily contact. This may unfold in family relationships marked by longstanding conflict, or in friendships that bring persistent pain. Even when the physical or emotional separation feels heavy, the boundary honours the sanctity of both lives. Through prayer and patient goodwill, the connection remains, even if through silence or space.

 ## Jesus' Example of Boundaries

Jesus modelled boundaries as a natural expression of unhindered love. In His conversation with the rich young ruler, Jesus offered both invitation and challenge: *"Go, sell all you have,"* He said, touching the heart of the young man's struggle. When the ruler walked away sad, Jesus let him go. He did not chase after him or plead, but held His boundary, allowing choice and growth to unfold. With the Pharisees, Jesus spoke candid truth, refusing false unity or participation in hypocrisy. Each interaction pulsed with grace and wisdom, never veering toward enabling or harshness. His boundaries were not walls of rejection but doors of clarity, pointing people toward freedom and accountability.

Healthy boundaries do not diminish courage; they create room for it. Secure in God's love, believers step more confidently into roles that require strength, brave kindness, and self-sacrifice. When personal limits are respected, energy and hope return, making acts of restoration not just a possibility but a living rhythm in home, workplace, and community. Proper boundaries anchor relationships, preparing hearts for even greater expressions of love.
To establish boundaries is to recognise the dignity of both you and others. It is an acknowledgment that God has given each of us responsibility over our hearts, our choices, and our obedience.

Without boundaries, relationships easily drift into imbalance, resentment, or burnout. With boundaries, however, relationships flourish because love is given freely, not forced or manipulated. In setting healthy limits, you declare that your ultimate allegiance is to God's will, not to the pressure of people's demands.

Boundaries also preserve purpose. Jesus knew the urgency of His mission, and He often withdrew from the crowds to pray, rest, and realign with the Father. Those moments of retreat were not selfish but sacred, replenishing His strength so that He could pour Himself out again. In the same way, when believers choose to honour their God-given capacity, they ensure longevity in their calling. They guard against exhaustion and keep their hearts tender, ready to serve with joy rather than compulsion.

Ultimately, boundaries are an act of faith. They trust that God is in control, not our constant striving or our need to please others. They remind us that love flourishes best within order, clarity, and truth. When we set boundaries in God's wisdom, we create spaces where His presence can dwell richly, and where love can be expressed in its purest form without manipulation, fear, or exhaustion.

 ## Love-Fuelled Courage

Healthy boundaries make room for deeper connections by keeping love sincere and focused rather than scattered or drained. When believers guard their hearts with wisdom, they become free to love more courageously. Love, rooted securely in God's grace, transforms self-preservation into an active, outward impulse. Instead of clinging to safety, it becomes possible to move into situations that require vulnerability. This is the starting point for love that acts boldly for God's kingdom, even when the risk carries uncertainty.

Mind His Business Not Theirs

 Fearless Compassion

Love grounded in God's acceptance equips people to approach the world with compassion that refuses to retreat in the face of rejection or discomfort. The apostle John wrote, Where love pervades, fear cannot dominate. The possibility of not being liked, understood, or accepted loses the power to dictate choices.

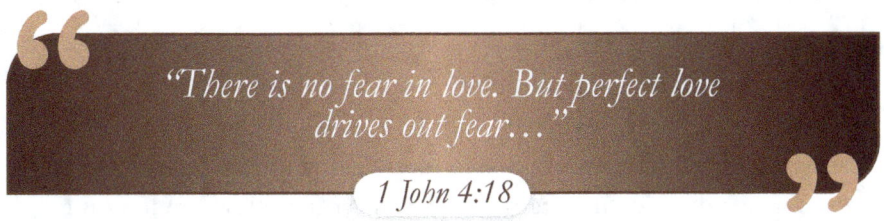

"There is no fear in love. But perfect love drives out fear..."

1 John 4:18

A professional may sense a coworker in crisis and feel prompted to reach out, even at the risk of social awkwardness or being brushed off. When God's love has saturated the heart, compassion overcomes hesitation. A believer visits a neighbour stricken with grief, not because of guarantees of a warm reception, but because love refuses to leave suffering unanswered. When a business owner chooses honesty during a difficult negotiation, even at the potential cost of profits, love is working beyond fear of loss. In these moments, the risk is real, but love views any failure as an opportunity to learn, mature, and trust God at a deeper level. Even when the outcome is unpredictable, love interprets "failure" as another step in growing in Christlike courage.

 Initiating Reconciliation

Disagreements, betrayals, and misunderstandings are unavoidable in any context. God's love does not shelter believers from relational pain, yet it dissolves pride and self-justification that leads to avoidance.

Jesus taught, Love motivates action, not passivity. The one empowered by love refuses to wait for the other party to make the first move.

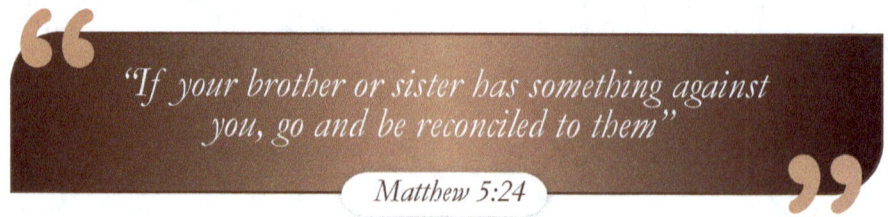

> "If your brother or sister has something against you, go and be reconciled to them"
>
> Matthew 5:24

Consider a ministry team fractured by miscommunication.
A member, convicted by love, picks up the phone to apologise for harsh words, stating the desire for peace over personal vindication. In a family where siblings have grown distant, one reaches out with an invitation to dinner, despite years of silence and unresolved tension. Love values humility more than being proven right. The effort can break destructive patterns, opening new conversation and healing where pride had built walls. Love invests in reconciliation even when results take time or initial attempts are rebuffed; the willingness to make the first move alone carries kingdom significance.

 ## Stepping Out in Faith

The assurance of God's unwavering love sets the foundation for obedience that is not paralysed by doubt or the unknown. Scripture records countless acts of ordinary people, secure in God's acceptance, who responded to God's call with practical steps, trusting Him for the outcome.

In the workplace, a manager feels God's nudge to champion a marginalised employee despite possible pushback from peers. Church members hear a call to start a food pantry, pooling resources not knowing if support will last or how needs will grow. Entrepreneurs sense an irresistible urge to infuse business practices with biblical integrity, declining shortcuts despite external pressure to sacrifice values.

Mind His Business Not Theirs

In each case, the driver is not the promise of immediate results, but the confidence that God's love is real regardless of outcome. This sort of faith does not ignore practical challenges or prudent planning, but it refuses paralysis. Obedience becomes an offering rather than a transaction.

Courage Multiplication

Acts of love-driven bravery rarely stay confined to one person. They ripple outward, multiplying momentum within a community. The single teacher who refuses to overlook bullying, even when it costs rapport with colleagues, inspires students to defend the vulnerable. One church member's willingness to start a prayer group in a secular office encourages others to step beyond cultural hesitation. In a family, one person's honest confession and request for forgiveness becomes the seed for broader reconciliation among relatives.

When believers act boldly out of the abundance of God's love, onlookers' pickup courage themselves. Scripture is filled with these cascading effects, as when the early church, emboldened by the Spirit, watched the boldness of Peter and John and found their own voices (Acts 4:13). Courage, once modelled, is often contagious. Communities form around a shared willingness to act in love, launching projects, ministries, or reforms that would seem overwhelming if attempted alone. The result is not only a chain-reaction of action, but an environment in which God's kingdom can expand through the collective strength of those transformed by love.

Concluding Thoughts

Now that we understand how to move from receiving God's love to actively expressing it through kindness, healing, boundaries, and courage, we are equipped to live out our faith powerfully in every area of life. This is not a passive reception of divine affection, but an active partnership with the heart of God. When love takes root in us, it becomes a living force that spills over into everything we touch. It reshapes the way we speak, the way we serve, and the way we persevere through trials.

Embracing this transformative journey enables us to become vessels of the Father's love, impacting relationships, workplaces, and communities with intentional and practical acts rooted in grace. Love ceases to be an abstract ideal and instead becomes a visible expression of God's presence through us. In moments of conflict, love chooses peace. In moments of opportunity, love chooses generosity. In moments of fear, love chooses courage. This rhythm of divine expression is what marks the life of a believer who has moved beyond receiving into releasing.

As we cultivate daily habits of love-fuelled action, habits of prayer, reflection, generosity, forgiveness, and service, our lives begin to align more closely with Christ's own example. These practices are not simply spiritual disciplines, but the scaffolding that sustains a life of faith in the midst of a noisy and often distracted world. When combined with wise boundaries, such habits guard our energy and direct our focus, ensuring that our love remains pure, steady, and resilient.

In this way, we prepare ourselves for deeper expressions of God's kingdom influence. A heart rooted in God's love becomes both a sanctuary for healing and a launching pad for transformation. This foundation not only renews our own hearts, drawing us into greater intimacy with the Father, but also invites others into the hope and restoration found in Christ. Our presence becomes a testimony, a quiet but powerful invitation for others to taste and see that the Lord is good.

As we continue to walk this path, we set the stage for even greater growth, influence, and service. We become participants in God's unfolding story, bringing light into dark places and embodying the very kingdom we proclaim. Each act of kindness, each courageous stand for truth, each boundary upheld in wisdom, all of these are seeds sown into eternity. And as they take root, they prepare the way for God's kingdom to flourish more fully, both in us and through us, until the whole world is filled with the knowledge of His glory.

KEY 8

FINISHING WELL – YOUR REWARD FROM HIS BUSINESS

True success isn't measured by trophies, promotions, or applause it's measured by faithfulness, integrity, and acts that echo into eternity. Daily choices matter more than public recognition. Small, unseen acts of love, prayer & service carry eternal weight

Philip Dada Jr

Mind His Business Not Theirs

Most people believe that a successful life is measured by visible accomplishments, promotions, awards, or public recognition. Yet, these achievements often leave a deeper longing unfulfilled and fade quickly from memory. The idea that lasting significance depends on external success is not only misleading but blinds us to a far greater truth: the real rewards lie beyond what this world can offer. What if the true measure of your life's impact isn't in trophies or titles, but in unseen acts that echo eternally? This chapter challenges the common pursuit of approval and invites a shift in perspective that aligns daily choices with God's eternal purposes. It calls for a redefinition of success, one rooted in faithfulness, integrity, and a mission that transcends time. Here lies an invitation to live with enduring intention, embracing every season with steadfast hope and joy, knowing that how we finish matters more than how we begin or even how we progress.

 ## The Reality of Eternal Perspective

Chasing after what the world praises can draw anyone into a cycle of effort that never quite satisfies. In the workplace, it's easy to measure success by promotions, awards, or financial gain. Long hours promise advancement, but each accomplishment soon fades, replaced by new pressures and fresh goals. Church leaders might pour themselves into visible ministries, preaching, singing, teaching, hoping to be recognised for their dedication. Yet applause dies down, and the fulfilment of being noticed soon grows thin. Business professionals watch sales numbers and profits, and while milestones feel significant in the moment, they quickly lose their shine as targets move, and expectations rise.

By contrast, investments in what God values bear significance that circumstance can never erase. Prayer for a struggling coworker, forgiveness offered to a difficult family member, or showing up faithfully to a low-profile ministry role, these may not make headlines or earn recognition at work, but they shape a legacy that lasts.

Acts rooted in love, the patient cultivation of kindness, generosity that seeks no payback, these are seeds sown toward a harvest that far outlives earthly achievements. Obedience to God's gentle direction brings changes, both seen and unseen, that ripple out past the boundaries of today.

Shaping one's life for eternal reward takes a shift in mindset. Instead of measuring a day by how much was checked off a list, meaning flows from asking if this day was lived in faith and faithfulness. Priorities align around what pleases God, not popular opinion or fleeting opportunity. In business, integrity and service become more important than reputation or the next deal. In family, loving well and modelling grace carries more weight than matching societal standards of success. Decisions, large or small, find direction when filtered through the question, "How will this matter in the light of eternity?"

Scripture teaches a principle often called "heavenly accounting." God keeps track of things no one else sees or celebrates. Jesus highlighted the widow's small coin, not the wealthy donors' gifts. Every quiet act of faith, each honest effort, each prayer behind closed doors, these do not disappear. In God's eyes, significance is not tied to size, style, or audience. A volunteer preparing chairs before a prayer meeting, a professional refusing to cut corners in a transaction, a parent tending to children's spiritual growth, for God, none of this is wasted labour. He weighs the heart's intention and faithfulness, not an unbroken record of perfection.

This approach brings new motivation for perseverance in discouraging seasons. When effort seems small or results go unseen, the knowledge that God notices provide lasting encouragement. During years of ministry that bear little visible fruit or careers that progress less quickly because of ethical standards, Christians can find strength in knowing it is consistency, showing up, loving well, and trusting God for outcomes, that God values. The applause of heaven does not sound louder for those who appear successful, but for those who are steadfast, truthful, and obedient. Daily purpose becomes clearer when it connects with eternal destiny. Those who understand their true citizenship lies in God's kingdom see every moment as part of a bigger picture.

A nurse who cares tirelessly for patients, an accountant bringing order and honesty to finances, or a manager investing in the growth of employees, all carry out divine purposes in ordinary tasks. Joy emerges in even the repetitive or difficult when each act is seen as service to God, a way to further His redemption in the world. This sets apart the difference between endless busyness and a grounded life. Faith-inspired action breathes hope into routine, pulling every decision into alignment with something that truly matters.

Trials and setbacks do not defeat those anchored in immortal hope. Disappointments, losses, and delays will come, often uninvited and unexplainable. Yet, clinging to the promise of eternal life brings unshakable resilience. Paul's words in 2 Corinthians remind believers that present struggles are "light and momentary" compared to the "eternal weight of glory" waiting for them. Stories abound of Christians who laboured without applause, endured suffering, or stood alone, and yet remained steadfast because the assurance of Christ's reward never runs dry. Gratitude and perseverance flourish in soil watered by hope beyond circumstances.

Seeking to finish well invites honest examination of motives and ambition. An eternal perspective frees believers from living for human approval. Ambitions realign, not stirred by applause, but directed by the desire for God's pleasure. Every goal, every act of service, every leadership choice shifts toward honouring Christ, paving the way for a life defined not by what others applaud, but by what delights the Father's heart.

 ## Motives That Please the Father

Recognition from others can quickly become a hidden trap, drawing attention to itself even while doing good. In the office, a congratulatory email can spark the urge to outperform peers for praise rather than purpose. Within the church, applause for a moving testimony may create the subtle temptation to mould future service around what receives affirmation. This craving for validation, while seemingly harmless, steadily shifts the aim of ambition. Rather than focusing on God's pleasure, efforts are redirected toward applause, awards, or social approval.

The result is a measured emptiness. Actions may appear spiritual from the outside, but the heart experiences unrest and a quiet anxiety, constantly measuring itself against what can be seen rather than what is truly worthwhile. Desiring to be known or celebrated is common, often beginning with good intentions. Yet, it soon grows into a pattern of seeking fulfilment in likes, compliments, or promotions. This affects not only personal contentment but also weakens spiritual vision. The more one reaches for public recognition, the fainter God's quiet commendation becomes. A children's ministry worker may overextend themselves for acknowledgment. A manager might devote long hours for a performance review rather than the pursuit of justice and care for employees. When motives intermingle, they dilute faithfulness. Spiritual energy is spent chasing approval, and the soul eventually stagnates, left unsatisfied by temporary applause.

Real-life faith brings daily tests of motive. Consider the act of serving at a local shelter. One volunteer feels joy in the silent reward of making a difference. Another, though earnestly helpful, looks for subtle cues of appreciation, a thank you, a mention from the pulpit, a spot in the newsletter. The difference is internal, but the impact is immense. Mixed motives slowly erode intimacy with God, building habits of self-promotion where humility and sincerity should thrive. Over time, the relentless pursuit of external approval leaves behind spiritual fatigue and an uneasy sense that all is not as it should be.

A greater invitation stands before every follower of Christ: to seek God's "well done" as the highest achievement. This shift transforms ambition. Desire is no longer defined by public success or admiration but by a quiet determination to please the Father in every circumstance. A teacher who chooses honesty when tempted to inflate student scores, a business leader who forsakes a lucrative contract rather than compromise integrity, a parent quietly sacrificing for their children, these all embody the strength and peace that flow from living for God's approval. The outcome is not always visible. Sometimes, kingdom values push believers away from centre stage. But in obscurity, character is refined, and enduring satisfaction settles in. Unseen acts of obedience take on profound spiritual significance. When someone gives generously to a neighbour in secret, or prays faithfully behind closed doors, eternity witnesses what earthly eyes ignore.

In the workplace, an employee cleans up after others even when no one is watching. A friend forgives a wrong without fanfare, holding no bitterness. These private moments of faithfulness are precious to God. He regards the sincere over the spectacular, the honest over the highly regarded. Embracing the unseen fosters humility, freeing believers from comparison and strengthening devotion. Service becomes sincere, not strategic.

Sustaining pure motives requires more than self-awareness. Intentional habits must anchor hearts, steering actions back to their true purpose. Setting aside regular times for prayer focused on motive, asking God to sift the desires beneath each decision, develops spiritual clarity. Engaging trusted friends or mentors as accountability partners provides a protective measure.

These relationships offer gentle challenges and honest conversations that keep ambitions aligned with God's values. Using scripture as a mirror is crucial. Passages such as Psalm 139, inviting God to "search my heart," or 1 Corinthians 10:31, urging that everything be done for God's glory, help assess intentions in daily routines. Before a big meeting, a quick reflection on Colossians 3:23 guides professionals toward wholehearted, Christ-oriented service rather than empty ambition.

These practices work in every sphere. In business, a leader might pause each morning, seeking to serve rather than impress. In parenting, moments of honest prayer take precedence over striving for visible "success." Church ministries flourish when planners and volunteers value God's reward above spotlight. Such rhythms train the soul to treasure what outlasts applause, recalibrating priorities toward genuine faithfulness.

Every day, motives shape actions. When driven by a longing for God's approval, quiet moments teem with lasting significance. This mindset gradually lays the foundation for a legacy not only of achievement, but of transformative influence that echoes far beyond a single lifetime.

Leaving a Ripple Effect

Jesus's teaching turns every measure of legacy upside down. He said that *"whoever loses their life for His sake will actually find it."* From the earliest believers to today's church, every person who has left footprints of faith has done so by living for more than their own story. A self-preserving life closes doors to lasting impact. This may appeal to our desire for safety and predictability, but it slowly erodes our potential. The kingdom of God grows when believers dare to reach beyond comfort, pour out their resources, and put others ahead of themselves. Examples from scripture and church history show that meaning and purpose never grow in the soil of self-protection. A mother who chooses to nurture her children's faith in small, nearly invisible daily acts does more to change the world than one who seeks applause or security. A business leader who sacrifices profit to treat every employee with dignity shows the power of eternal thinking, leaving a workplace legacy that blesses countless families. Comfort eventually ends with the person enjoying it, but sacrifice multiplied by God carries on for generations.

Discipling the next generation stands at the centre of all enduring influence. This is where faithfulness echoes longest. Every time a mentor invests in the spiritual maturity of a younger believer, the results stretch beyond a single life. Within church communities, older believers can walk alongside newer Christians, modelling prayer, perseverance, and humility. A seasoned professional at work can support a young colleague, teaching them to keep Christ at the heart of every decision. In families, a parent who takes time after a long day to discuss God's faithfulness writes a living testament that shapes not only children, but their grandchildren. The method of discipleship multiplies what no single person alone could accomplish. Moses groomed Joshua, who in turn led Israel forward. Paul poured into Timothy, forming pillars who upheld the church after Paul's departure. Faith passed from life to life weaves a tapestry that holds the church strong across centuries. The legacy of one can anchor the faith of many. Investing in others is demanding. It may require letting go of control, reducing personal productivity, or enduring rejection. The fruit, however, is visible in the resilience of faith communities, in the steady growth of new leaders, and in the vibrant worship of generations who might never have known Christ apart from faithful mentoring.

The willingness to celebrate others' victories also marks a life that points toward eternity. Christian legacy thrives when we freely encourage and champion others rather than clutching recognition. Envy, competition, and the need to be first, block God's blessing and shrink our reach. Jesus offered dignity to others, lifted up the lowly, and spoke life into those treated as outcasts. A ministry leader who steps aside so a gifted young pastor can preach sends a signal that the mission matters more than personal status. A parent who cheers when their child's talent outshines their own lays a foundation of security and purpose. Imagine a workplace where a team leader nominates an employee for an industry award, then publicly affirms their leadership in front of others. This humility not only empowers the recipient but sets a culture where every contribution is counted and new ideas flourish. When we release control and give away glory, others grow boldly, and the reach of our faith extends further than we could ever imagine alone.

Recording testimonies offers a powerful way to build legacy and nurture faith in others. Every story of God's faithfulness becomes a spiritual inheritance. Begin by collecting moments, big and small, where God's presence became clear in your journey. This may include answered prayers, unexpected provision, restored relationships, or specific words from scripture that carried you through trouble. Write these stories in a notebook or capture them using audio and video recordings. Organise them by season of life, significant events, or central themes such as healing, guidance, or forgiveness. Once gathered, find natural ways to share them. Read them at family gatherings or write a letter to your children. Share them at church meetings or publish short reflections through online posts or podcasts. For example, a woman recalls sharing her journey of chronic illness and prayer with her grandchildren. Years later, as her granddaughter faces her own health struggles, she remembers God's provision in her grandmother's life and draws courage to pray and trust. The shared story not only strengthens an individual faith but ripples out, forming anchors of hope and guidance for a wider community.

Self-Help Exercise: Discipling the Next Generation

- Identify a younger person in your sphere, child, colleague, or church member, who desires to grow in faith or life skills.
- Schedule a regular, short meeting with them, such as a weekly conversation or shared activity.
- Choose one area to focus on: prayer, reading scripture, integrity at work, or serving others.
- Ask questions and listen first; encourage them to voice their hopes and challenges.
- Model the behaviour or practice you want to pass on through your own daily actions.
- Pray for them by name and invite them to join you in prayer.
- Offer honest encouragement and feedback, affirming both effort and progress.
- Repeat these steps consistently over several weeks or months.
-

For instance, a teacher at work invites a new employee to lunch each Wednesday. They discuss challenges, talk through scriptures that speak into work-life tensions, and pray for each other's needs. Over time, the younger colleague grows in confidence and maturity, eventually mentoring someone else. The cycle of faith and influence continues, rooted in small seeds of deliberate investment.

Legacies that last, those reaching over generations, require persistent, God-centred choices in every season of giving and serving.

 ### Celebrating the Race, Not Just the Finish

Building something that lasts begins not just with outward testimony or legacy, but with the inward choices made in the quiet moments of everyday faith. Though many measure a life's worth by dramatic milestones, a vibrant spiritual legacy is shaped in how believers embrace the ordinary seasons in-between. Gratitude and joy become both the posture and the fuel for daily living, sustaining perseverance even when the finish line seems far ahead.

Appreciating each step along the journey is not an emotional luxury but a vital spiritual practice. Gratitude for small victories recalibrates attention from what is missing to what is already present. When a believer thanks God for the patience shown during a frustrating conversation, the gentle word spoken to a difficult coworker, or the discipline to rise early for prayer, their eyes open to God's faithfulness at work right now. One might recall an exhausted parent whispering thanks for a child's unexpected hug at bedtime or a teacher quietly rejoicing as a struggling student grasps a challenging concept. These moments may seem minor, yet pausing to recognise and appreciate them breathes contentment into the routine. Thanksgiving for what is easily overlooked becomes an antidote to discouragement, especially in seasons when grand achievements are out of reach. Over time, these acts of gratitude forge resilience, making it possible to press on with hope through the slow, unseen chapters of growth.

Joy, then, is cultivated not merely by dramatic breakthroughs but as a deep wellspring rooted in God's consistent presence. This joy is accessible in the middle of a hectic commute, while folding laundry, or serving unnoticed at a local shelter. A disciple might savour a quiet morning with a cup of coffee and scripture, receiving joy that arises not from circumstance but from the simple nearness of God. There is a certain delight found when someone prepares a meal for a neighbour without any recognition, or when an exhausted volunteer finds unexpected laughter in conversation with others at a church event. These glimpses of gladness in mundane tasks reaffirm that faith is not just preparation for the future but is to be lived and relished in the present. Remaining anchored in today's opportunities for rejoicing guards against the temptation to postpone happiness until some distant spiritual achievement is reached. Authentic spiritual maturity grows as believers learn to discover purpose and meaning, not only when standing on mountaintops, but also when faithfully traversing quiet valleys.

Comparison, however, threatens to dull both gratitude and joy, whispering that one's journey is less valuable when measured against another's. In community life, it is easy to notice the ministry leader with a larger platform, the family whose children seem more spiritually together, or the coworker whose prayers sound eloquent and powerful. This habit of looking sideways breeds' discontent. When a young professional compares their slow progress with the rapid success of a mentor, or a newly married couple measures their rhythms of connection against those seen on social media, envy and insecurity often follow. Choosing instead to focus on the uniqueness of one's calling releases believers from the pressure of imitation. Embracing God's hand in a story that looks different from others replaces striving with peace. Honesty about personal struggles and celebration of others' victories allow authenticity to flourish. Rather than competing for significance, believers begin to honour the distinct paths God has carved out for each of them, strengthening the bonds of Christian community and personal identity.

Maintaining spiritual rhythms of rest shapes a healthy and enduring faith. Sabbath is not merely a religious relic or a rigid weekly appointment but a living invitation to step out of constant activity and remember one's dependence on God. Rest can appear as a quiet hour set aside in the middle of a workweek, a family meal free from technology, or a short walk in nature to listen and reflect. Practical Sabbath habits are possible even for the busiest professional or ministry leader. A business executive may block out moments in the calendar for prayerful reflection before meetings. A parent might institute a "no chores" night to enjoy playful time with children or a quiet evening of worship music. These purposeful pauses recalibrate mind and spirit, pushing back against the relentless demands of production and performance. Rest signals trust in God's sufficiency, freeing believers to approach their callings with renewed creativity and compassion rather than burnout. It is not weakness but wisdom, a way to honour the body and soul as gifts from God.

Rooted in practices of gratitude, joy, authenticity, and rest, believers remain set apart from the world's frantic pace and passing rewards. Each decision to savour today, to celebrate small progress, and to honour God's timing becomes part of a larger story that stretches into eternity. When these rhythms mark the unfolding journey, ordinary days become the very ground on which steadfastness is tested, and spiritual inheritance grows.

 ## Faithful unto the End

The journey of consecration begins with learning to delight in the presence of God, but it matures when appreciation shapes every season into an opportunity for enduring faithfulness. Champions of spiritual purpose possess a unique ability to savour the present without losing sight of the finish line. This appreciation infuses even ordinary routines with gratitude, allowing believers to transform daily experiences into offerings of devotion. Yet as the years press on and responsibilities shift, a core challenge emerges, how to sustain mission and consecration all the way to the end, when energy may wane and distractions multiply.

Devoted believers in every arena of life, those shepherding teams, navigating workplaces, or guiding ministries, face moments where perseverance feels costly. The significance of finishing strong rises in these moments. To finish strong means more than just avoiding moral failure; it calls for a life marked by consistent energy, clear focus, and unwavering trust in God's calling. Fixing attention on eternal goals each day creates the conditions for perseverance. This focus makes burdens seem lighter, because every task gains lasting meaning. For example, a seasoned teacher who views each class session as a deposit into students' souls finds fresh strength for daily challenges, motivated by a vision larger than immediate results.

Sustaining this kind of lifelong zeal grows out of well-chosen spiritual habits. Purposeful disciplines, woven into the structure of daily life, protect mission from exhaustion. Scheduled prayer anchors hearts in God's promises and priorities, providing a place to pour out anxieties and receive new direction. Carving out specific times for prayer transforms vague good intentions into concrete commitment. Accountability and partnerships bring needed perspective, especially in seasons of fatigue.

Meeting regularly with a trusted friend or mentor offers a safe space to process hard questions, invite correction, and seek encouragement. Intentional reflection on spiritual victories, perhaps through journaling or storytelling, reminds believers of God's faithfulness already displayed. A retired business owner might recall moments when God supplied at just the right time, infusing current struggles with fresh hope.

Spiritual momentum often depends as much on relationships as on personal resolve. Having wise mentors and faithful companions creates an environment where encouragement and correction thrive. A study group or prayer partnership, formed in pursuit of spiritual growth, becomes a lifeline in times of discouragement or confusion. When setbacks come, encouragers help reinterpret struggles as stepping stones, pointing out the growth that the weary believer may not see. Consider a physician approaching the final years of her career, wrestling with doubts about her lasting influence. A mentor's words, reminding her of hundreds of lives touched over decades, rekindle purpose for her remaining service, reminding her that legacy is built patiently. Prayer partners who meet over coffee or video chat may share burdens, celebrate answered prayers, and challenge one another to remain steadfast. These connections guard against isolation and drift, making perseverance a shared venture instead of a lonely obligation.

Anticipation of eternity fuels resilience in the face of suffering or delay. Living with the end in view lends hope during life's darkest valleys. When the prospect of reunion with the Father stands clear, momentary disappointments take on a hopeful perspective. Believers who fix their eyes on heaven embrace a defiant joy that transcends circumstances. A farmer who knows his labour leads toward an eternal harvest endures drought or poor seasons with patience beyond mere optimism. A widow, longing for reunion with lost loved ones, chooses generosity and kindness as acts of hope rather than withdrawal. The anticipation of eternal fellowship with God turns pain into preparation, sorrow into seeds of future joy. This hope keeps purpose alive and releases believers from the grip of present anxieties.

The ultimate fruit of unwavering obedience is a legacy that inspires generations long after this life ends. Consistent obedience, displayed in public decisions and unseen sacrifices, writes a story others will read. Observers and followers watch the one who refuses shortcuts, forgives when wronged, and prays without ceasing. A grandfather's humble integrity, expressed in quiet service and steadfast faith, becomes a model for grandchildren and neighbours alike. Gathering each Sunday, his family speaks of his honest business dealings and gentle words, drawing strength to walk in faith themselves.

A faithful life becomes a living letter, its message echoing in communities, workplaces, and homes for years to come. The impact multiplies as mentees, children, coworkers, and friends carry forward the pattern they have witnessed. A community leader who quietly influences young professionals through authentic mentorship seeds future believers' devotion. By stewarding every season with purpose, believers set a pace others can follow, making the ultimate mark that outlives any single accomplishment. Through this mindset, every act of obedience becomes an eternal investment, and the journey's end promises the joy of hearing, "Well done, good and faithful servant."

 Final Thoughts

Now that we understand the power of adopting an eternal perspective, we can choose to live each day with purpose rooted in God's approval rather than fleeting applause. By aligning our motives with what truly pleases the Father, we lay the foundation for a legacy that not only honours Him but shapes generations to come. Embracing every season, whether filled with visible success or quiet service, with joy and gratitude strengthens our resolve to persevere faithfully until the end. This mindset transforms routine tasks into meaningful acts of worship, encourages sincere discipleship, and equips us to face challenges with resilient hope. As we commit to these truths, we step confidently into our calling as faithful stewards of the kingdom, investing in what lasts beyond this life and inspiring others to do the same.

CONCLUSION

As we come to the end of this journey, let's return to where it all began with a clear and passionate vision for who you are in God's story. The heartbeat of this book has always been to awaken you to the deep love of the Father, to help you rediscover your royal inheritance as His child, to call you to set apart your life for His purposes, to open your mind to a new kingdom way of thinking, and to send you forth, equipped and inspired to make an unmistakable difference wherever He places you. Every chapter has been designed not just to inform you but to provide practical tools for living intentionally, so you can step confidently into your unique assignment and reflect the Father's love in every sphere of life. This is not merely about absorbing ideas; it's about leaving behind passive learning and embracing the privilege of active participation in God's eternal work. When you look back over the ground we've covered together, you can see how each theme builds upon the last, forming a roadmap for authentic Christian living. We began by exploring the core truth of God's fatherhood, a love that is unconditional, pursuing, and restorative. This is where all true transformation starts: knowing you are fully accepted and deeply valued by the One who made you. From there, we moved into the recovery of royal identity. You learned to reject lies and limitations from past wounds or worldly pressures, standing instead in the dignity and authority Christ secured for you.

Consecration then became the next step, not as a rigid set of rules, but as an ongoing posture of surrender and devotion. Here, we saw that setting yourself apart is not about isolation from the world, but about being empowered to influence it with purity and purpose. The renewal of your mindset followed, inviting you to recognise how the world shapes perspectives around fear, scarcity, and competition, while the kingdom calls us to think with abundance, faith, and generosity. As you let go of limiting beliefs and embrace kingdom thinking, your actions begin to change from the inside out. Excellence entered the conversation as more than simple achievement; it became a reflection of God's character through your daily work, whether in a church, a business, an office, or a creative space. To bear witness to God's glory is to bring your best, empowered not by striving but by the Spirit's enabling grace.

Mind His Business Not Theirs

And as these foundations were laid, we discussed how to show up with integrity and faithfulness even in challenging, sometimes hostile, environments. In this way, excellence becomes a powerful act of worship, and your influence becomes a testimony to those watching.

Throughout this journey, love, active, courageous, sacrificial love, remained at the centre. Manifesting the Father's heart is about much more than personal morality; it's about drawing others to Him by the way you serve, forgive, encourage, and persevere. All of these elements: identity, consecration, mindset, action, and love, are woven together, creating an integrated approach to kingdom living. It's not a checklist, but a dynamic, holistic process that equips you to embody the gospel in every area of your life. As you reflect on what has spoken most powerfully to you, I hope you will carry forward several breakthrough realisations. First, remember that worldly success fades, but a life anchored in God's purpose is both fulfilling and eternally significant. Shifting from performance-driven approval or orphan-hearted striving to beloved sonship changes everything, it frees you to live from acceptance, not for it. Each day presents a choice: legalistic striving or surrendered intimacy. Transformation flows when you choose to surrender and seek deeper closeness with God rather than perfectionism.
You have learned to renew your thinking, to place kingdom priorities above self-centred ambitions, and to align your thoughts with truth, hope, and faith. Excellence, now for you, is no longer about proving worth but about expressing gratitude for your calling. Maintaining integrity and godly influence amidst pressure is possible, and it brings lasting impact. Even when circumstances are difficult or misunderstood, you can express courageous love and kindness, because your ultimate validation comes from God alone. These shifts move you beyond theoretical knowledge into a robust, mature faith that stands firm and inspires others.

It is important to pause and celebrate the commitment you've already shown. Engaging honestly with deep spiritual truths requires humility and bravery, especially when facing themes like inner healing, boundary-setting, ethical dilemmas, or perseverance through adversity. Choosing to finish a book like this is no small feat, it marks your willingness to grow, to be stretched, and to invest in your own transformation.

Mind His Business Not Theirs

Consider this a victory in itself. Your dedication is laying the foundation for a life brimming with meaning and purpose, and your progress deserves recognition. Let that encouragement fuel your confidence to continue walking boldly in your calling. Transformation is a lifelong pursuit, and the path ahead is full of new opportunities. To sustain momentum, commit now to developing daily rhythms of surrender, and finding moments to realign your heart and invite God's guidance. Prioritise time in scripture, allowing His word to reshape your perspective continually. Seek community: trusted friends, mentors, and faith groups who will push you toward accountability, growth, and joy. Look for ways to practice kindness and pursue excellence in whatever roles you occupy, in the boardroom, in your family, in your neighbourhood. Set tangible goals that reflect your sense of assignment, and don't hesitate to seek out further resources, join a small group, or find a mentor to walk beside you.

Stepping into this mission is not meant to be a solitary venture. One of the best ways to deepen your own growth is to share what you've experienced. Tell your story to those closest to you. Model courage, love, and unwavering integrity at work or at home, knowing that silent witness can draw others to the Father's heart even before words are spoken. Join others in communities of practice, church teams, small groups, service organisations, where mission and growth are shared values. When you live outwardly what you've learned inwardly, your impact multiplies far beyond your individual reach.

Before we part ways, I want to extend my deepest thanks to you. Thank you for trusting me to guide you through this transformative material. Your desire to pursue God's heart and fulfil your kingdom role matters, not just to you, but to your family, your workplace, your community, and the larger tapestry of God's unfolding story. My passion is simply to help you see how precious, needed, and powerful your assignment truly is. If you'd like to stay connected, learn more, or be encouraged along the way, I would be honoured to hear from you again in future resources or through my online spaces. Please know that you are valued, prayed for, and celebrated as part of this growing movement of kingdom-minded believers.

Finally, let's keep the eternal perspective front and centre. Everything you do in obedience, however small, carries weight that extends far beyond what you can see. The kingdom of God is advancing, and your contribution has enduring significance. Anchor your motivation in the promises yet to be fulfilled and the legacy you are building, one faithful step at a time. This hope will help sustain you through trials, disappointments, and seasons of waiting. So, as you close this book, make a deliberate decision not just to run your race, but to run it well. Refuse to be entangled by the familiar patterns of self-sabotage that once felt normal. Those hidden compromises, the subtle doubts, and the quiet settling, they are not your portion. You were made for more. Rise above the noise, the expectations, and the opinions of men that seek to define or diminish you. Their voices are fleeting, but God's call on your life is eternal.

Embrace every season with courage, knowing that your story is still unfolding, and your legacy is being forged through everyday acts of obedience and faithfulness. Surround yourself with wise mentors and companions who sharpen, stretch, and support you. Keep your eyes fixed on Jesus the author and finisher of your faith and run with anticipation for the reward that awaits when you stand before your Heavenly Father.

Yours is a calling worth living for and finishing strong.

Go forward with courage. Go forward with love. And above all, go with the unwavering assurance that you are on divine assignment, living for a purpose far greater than yourself. May your life shine as a brilliant reflection of the Father's grace, and may your journey inspire others to rise, to hope, and to walk boldly into their own redemption story.

Transformation is not a moment; it's a lifelong pursuit.
And the path ahead will demand intentionality. To stay aligned, you must establish daily rhythms of surrender. Choose moments to pause, reset, and invite God's guidance afresh. Let His Word renew your mind and shape your perspective, especially when culture, fear, or your past try to speak louder.

Surround yourself with community, faithful friends, mentors, and accountability that refuses to let you shrink back Whether you lead in the boardroom, serve in your home, or simply show up in your everyday spaces, walk in kindness, pursue excellence, and carry purpose with clarity.

Set goals that align with your divine calling. Don't hesitate to seek help, join a small group, reach out to a mentor, or invest in resources that fuel your growth. And when the temptation comes to compare, to perform, or to prove?

Remember this: Mind His business, not theirs.

Let that truth anchor you. Let it free you. Let it keep you.

Because your story redeemed, set apart, and anointed was never meant to blend in. It was meant to stand out, shine bright, and point others home.

ACKNOWKLEDGEMENTS

First and foremost, I give all glory and honour to God, my Father, my Creator, my Sustainer and to His only begotten Son Jesus, the matchless one, my one true love and the great king of Zion This book would not have been possible without His guidance, wisdom, and faithfulness. Every idea, insight, and word written within these pages is a reflection of His Spirit moving in my life, shaping my thoughts, and aligning my steps with His purposes.

I am deeply grateful to my wife, Caitlin, whose unwavering support, love, and encouragement have sustained me through the highs and lows of this journey. Your prayers, friendship, counsel, and partnership in life and ministry have been a source of strength beyond measure. It is an honour and joy point to partner with you for life.
I love you with my everything.

To my parents, whose faith, guidance, and belief in me laid the foundation for everything I am and continue to become, I say thank you. Your investment in my life through teaching, discipline, and example has shaped my character and instilled in me the values of diligence, integrity, and purpose.

I want to especially acknowledge my pastors, Peter Nembhard, and Carris Nembhard, for their love, guidance, and example, which have been a source of wisdom and encouragement since I have known them. I am also profoundly grateful to my best friend, Michael Olasope, a man of steel who has been by my side in every season and makes me feel accompanied on this lonely road. Your friendship, loyalty, and honesty have been invaluable.

To the readers of this book, thank you for trusting me with your time and attention. It is my prayer that these pages will inspire you to live intentionally, embrace your divine assignment, and walk boldly in the fullness of God's calling for your life.

Finally, to the Holy Spirit, my constant companion and guide, thank you for leading, correcting, and empowering me to write with clarity, purpose, and boldness. May this book serve as a vessel for Your truth and transformative power in every life it touches.

ABOUT THE AUTHOR

Philip Dada Jr. is a devoted son of God, a loving husband, a passionate preacher of the gospel, a visionary entrepreneur, and a gifted menswear designer from Nigeria.

From an early age, Philip demonstrated an entrepreneurial spirit, starting with small ventures such as selling grilled meat during his secondary school days and designing unique school uniforms. His passion for creativity was evident, even as he pursued an LLB in Law at Coventry University, graduating with a 2:1 degree in 2016. He successfully qualified as a barrister and solicitor in 2021. Despite his legal background, Philip's love for fashion and tailoring inspired him to launch his namesake menswear brand, Philip Dada Jr (PDJ) in 2019.

Committed to excellence and innovation, he established a factory in Nigeria in 2021 and later opened the first studio in London in 2023. His brand quickly gained prominence, dressing notable footballers like Arsenal's Ian Wright for the Euro 2024, as well as various celebrities and influential men in society.

He is also the founder of Entrepreneurs Intercession, a prayer and equipping community for entrepreneurs, which is a fast-growing community drawing hundreds of entrepreneurs to prayer and building profitable businesses within different industries, globally.

Alongside his wife Caitlin, they lead the discipleship department at their local church within ARC Global. Philip's work is deeply rooted in his Christian faith, which informs a visionary and prophetic approach combined with practical application, all to the glory of Christ Jesus, His lover and king.

MIND HIS BUSINESS, NOT THEIRS

Mind His Business, Not Theirs is a bold call to break free from the self-sabotaging patterns, limiting beliefs, and approval-chasing that keep many Christians stuck, even while appearing successful. In a world obsessed with validation, performance, and public image, this book invites you to stop living for the opinions of men and start walking fully in the purpose God uniquely designed for you.

With clarity and conviction, this book introduces **eight transformative keys** that will help you shift from striving to surrender, from confusion to clarity, and from delay to divine momentum. These keys are not just concepts, they are spiritual tools that dismantle cycles of self-doubt, fear, and distraction, empowering you to align your life fully with the Father's business.

You'll begin by encountering the true nature of God as Father, breaking off distorted views shaped by culture or past wounds. You'll rediscover your identity not as someone earning approval, but as a beloved, called, and commissioned child of God. From that foundation, you'll learn how to overcome inner resistance and walk in lasting fruitfulness, stewarding your time, gifts, and voice with excellence.

This journey also leads you into **Kingdom mind mapping,** a renewal of thought that uproots toxic narratives and reorients your mind toward purpose and clarity. You'll be equipped to rise above societal pressure, cultural expectations, and the opinions that once held you back. Instead of reacting to the world, you'll respond to the call of God with confidence and boldness.

One of the book's central messages is that **excellence is worship,** not performance. You'll be challenged to complete your God-given assignments with integrity, creativity, and diligence, not to impress others, but to glorify the One who called you. By cultivating a deep partnership with the Holy Spirit, you'll learn how to navigate leadership, business, creativity, and relationships with divine strategy and supernatural peace.

This is more than a book. It's a **manual for movement, a framework for freedom,** and an **invitation to live unshackled** from fear, comparison, and compromise. Whether you're an entrepreneur, creative, professional, or leader, these pages will empower you to discern God's voice, execute His vision, and finish strong on His terms.

Mind His Business, Not Theirs will equip you to stop sabotaging your own progress, silence the noise of other people's expectations, and step fully into your divine assignment. It's time to stop watching others and start walking boldly in what God has specifically entrusted to you.

www.ingramcontent.com/pod-product-compliance
Lightning Source LLC
Chambersburg PA
CBHW071203070526
44584CB00019B/2904